FULLY INVESTED

Why Work-Life Balance Is a Total Lie

Other Books by the Author

Stress Free Money
Smart, Not Spoiled
Fit for Wealth
Beyond the Money
Wealth Wired Differently

FULLY INVESTED

Why Work-Life Balance Is a Total Lie

7 Strategies to Win Big
in Business and at Home

CHAD WILLARDSON

ethos
collective

Published by Igniting Souls
PO Box 43, Powell, OH 43065
IgnitingSouls.com

LCCN: 2025907329
Paperback ISBN: 978-1-63680-497-2
Hardback ISBN: 978-1-63680-498-9
eBook ISBN: 978-1-63680-499-6

Available in paperback, hardcover, e-book, and audiobook.

TABLE OF CONTENTS

INTRODUCTION

The Cost of Being Half-In

You've been told to "balance" work and life, as if you have two lives to keep from touching. You don't. You have *one life* to live. When you try to split life into separate compartments, you pay an expensive hidden tax—drift at home, distraction at work, guilt in both places. That's the cost of being half-in.

If I had to guess, in the last ninety days you've felt it: you care about winning big in business *and* being deeply present at home—and you're spread thin enough to question whether both are even possible. At the office, you get recognition and praise, so you double down. At home, you feel the distance and tell yourself you'll make it up "after the next big financial/business milestone is reached." Then the next milestone arrives. And the next.

Here's the truth most people won't say out loud: *work-life balance is a lie.*[IP] Not because home doesn't matter, but because "balance" treats your roles as competitors. They're not. When you live Fully Invested™, home and work don't compete; they *compound.*[IE] Your marriage fuels

Work-life balance is a lie.

your business growth and leadership. Your leadership blesses your marriage. Same person. Same standards. Different rooms.

I know the doubt that pops up when you read that. "Sounds nice, but in real life?" I get it. I founded and currently run multiple growing businesses while leading a busy family of seven. The answer isn't a 30-hour day. It's a different operating system—clear standards, clean calendar, protected attention, and the right people, systems, and rhythms that keep you aligned with your spouse and your business teams. I don't follow the "rules" that keep ambitious people stuck. I don't accept the premise that you must choose one or the other. And neither should you.

Imagine this: You finish a quarter at record revenue, *and* your spouse would describe you as present, connected, and fun. Your kids know what you stand for because they feel it daily. Your team moves faster with fewer fires because your standards are consistent everywhere you go. That picture isn't fantasy. It's what happens when you stop negotiating with your priorities and start leading an integrated life.

If you're not Fully Invested, you're settling. Settling looks respectable—good income, busy calendar—but it steals the life you actually want: extraordinary results, a strong marriage, and healthy, connected kids. You don't need to apologize for wanting all of it. You need a way to build all of it.

This book is that way. It's not theory. It's the framework, decision rules, and daily practices I use and teach—simple, repeatable moves that compound. You'll see how to:

- **Lead one life with one set of standards.** No "home Chad" vs. "work Chad."
- **Protect proximity.** Choose rooms and relationships that raise your standards and your character.
- **Win your calendar.** Design deep-work blocks and home rhythms that hold under pressure.
- **Delegate like a pro.** Hire, develop, and trust A-players so you stop wasting a $3,000 hour doing $30 tasks.
- **Strengthen the core.** Employ weekly spouse huddles, fast repair after conflict, and family rituals that anchor everyone.
- **Guard the gate.** Inputs drive outputs—curate what you watch, read, and who you follow.
- **Decide fast on people.** Have clear standards, use coaching when it's helpful, and clean exits when it isn't.
- **Measure what matters.** Track the few metrics that predict both revenue and relationship health.

And because skepticism is healthy, here's what Fully Invested is not:

- It's not perfection or an 18-hour hustle performance.
- It's not neglecting rest, family, faith, or health in the name of growth.
- It's not pretending conflict won't happen; it's learning fast repair so it doesn't compound.
- It's not balance by subtraction; it's alignment by design.

How to use this book: don't just nod along. Prove your commitment and beliefs with your new calendar. After each chapter, implement one move within 24 hours. Schedule a spouse huddle this week.

Block deep-work windows now. Text a mentor and upgrade a room you're in. Prune one energy drainer. Tiny, consistent deposits beat occasional heroic sprints.

You will be tempted to read, feel inspired, and drift back to default settings. Don't. Default is expensive. Presence is powerful. Integration is clarity. Alignment is profitable. The compounded life you want—elite results at work and genuine joy at home—sits on the other side of a decision: so be all in.

You get one life. Lead it *Fully Invested*—with the same standards in every room you enter. If you bring the ambition, I'll hand you the operating system. Let's build a life where your business wins, your marriage flourishes, and your kids are proud of the story you're writing—at the same time. Turn the page. Let's get to work.

EXCUSING SELF-SABOTAGE

I didn't find more hours—I took them back. I decided to stop doing the things that kept me from thriving at home and at work. Once I let those go, I had more time and more attention for what matters.

Most people pretend their wasted time doesn't exist. They'll say, "I can't possibly grow my business at a high level and be fully engaged with my family—I'm too slammed," but their screen-time and streaming history tell a much different story. What if you reclaimed twenty-five hours a week? That's *one thousand three hundred* hours this year. Imagine putting those extra hours into your business, your marriage, your kids, your health. Wouldn't that change your life?

If you feel yourself pushing back, saying, "He's not talking about me, I'm busy with important things," then lean in here. Your time-wasters might look different, but they usually land in the same places:

- Endless scrolling and aimless browsing
- TV/shows/streaming binges
- Consuming the daily news
- Meetings you didn't need to attend
- Constant email inbox checking
- Procrastination and indecision
- Busywork you should delegate
- Days with no clear priorities or plan

The common move is to hang on to these habits (the dopamine hits feel good) while chasing the fantasy of "work-life balance." Here's the reality: being half-in is very expensive. When you try to do everything without filters or boundaries you split your energy, and everything gets worse.

This book is about the opposite. Put a Fully Invested filter on your time and attention. Cut what doesn't serve your mission. Reclaim your hours. Aim them where you want to win: at home, at work, and at the same time.

Cut what doesn't serve your mission. Reclaim your hours.

Amber and Chad, 2001 (dating/engaged)

IT'S NOT 50-50

When my wife and I were engaged at BYU (at the young ages of 22 and 20), we took a Marriage Prep class from Professor Matthew Richardson. He told us, "If you think a great marriage is 50–50, your marriage will never work. It's 100–100." As a numbers guy, that initially confused me. How can it be 100–100? Over time, I learned: a husband and wife in a strong marriage don't split a fixed pie—they each bring their whole self to the relationship. This type of marriage commitment multiplies by two; it doesn't divide in half.

The same goes for your business and home life. When you try to split yourself, doing just enough in both, everything slips. You underperform, and you feel that low-grade guilt because you know you're not all-in. The answer is to be Fully Invested.

Now, let's be real: going all-in will sometimes burn you. I've committed to deals and opportunities that went sideways or didn't work out. Being Fully Invested does make you vulnerable, but it's worth it. Every failure or mistake taught me something I'll use for the rest of my life. I'd rather be Fully Invested and occasionally get bruised than play it safe, go half-in, and never come close to what was possible.

One thing I've learned along the way: detach your identity from the outcome of your effort. That's hard to do, but very important. I've had big wins and big losses. Being Fully Invested doesn't mean everything turns out perfectly; it means you live with clarity and courage either way. You're on a mission to make the most of your one life. You keep moving towards what you really want.

Years back, I began posting a lot of real-life, behind-the-scenes content on social media. The good, the bad, the ugly. Being my real self online without holding anything back. Initially, it was uncomfortable, but then I quickly realized that people are hungry for authenticity. When I was half-in, I posted safe, vanilla content and worried what people thought. It showed. Once I decided to be the real me in every setting, I let go of the naysayers and focused on where I'm headed.

Many along the way have asked me how I'm comfortable sharing my personal beliefs, opinions, struggles, and family life online, when it invites criticism and gossip. My answer is simple: I don't build my life around strangers' opinions.

Choose 100–100. Bring your whole self to your marriage and your business. Live Fully Invested—no half measures, no split standards, no pretending to be a different person at work, a different person at home, and a different person online or in social settings. Just be who you are, go after what matters, and keep going.

Amber and Chad, 2001

My husband and I have had pretty clear-cut roles from the beginning. One of the things we liked about each other when we were dating was that we both intended to have a rather traditional lifestyle.

As we began having children, I found that I really enjoyed being at home with them, and I was super lucky that I got to do exactly what I wanted.

Our roles don't compare. For us, teamwork means that we each take care of our areas of responsibility. We both perform at high levels in the areas where we feel passionate: my main area is our children, and now their spouses, and our grandchildren. Dane is passionate about his business and managing our resources.

For example, we have built three homes together, and we both understand what each other's jobs are as we build. He takes care of everything you can't see, like the plumbing, electrical, networking, insulation, etc., that makes the home function, and I take care of everything else, from the design to the details, that make the home livable.

Each of us taking care of our responsibilities empowers the other to continue with theirs.

–WENDY KIMBER,
LIFE COACH AND FOUNDER OF WENDY KIMBER COACHING

THE FINANCIAL SIDE

There are financial benefits of being Fully Invested too. Some people keep all their money sitting idle in savings rather than exposing themselves to the higher returns and risks of the markets. I don't believe in having big checking and savings account balances at all. I'm always Fully Invested, so our money's invested for growth at all times.

When you're not Fully Invested, there's a real opportunity cost. You're missing out on compound growth when you allow your money to sit around and gather dust. Entrepreneurs who exit their businesses often wonder what to do with the large lump sum they receive from the sale. It's tempting to "park" the money as cash or to invest it a little bit at a time over several years, because they don't know which way the market is headed.

Even though that sounds conservative, prudent, and thoughtful, all the financial investment studies show that over a ten-year time horizon or longer, you always would've been better off being Fully Invested right away, even if it seemed like it was a "bad" time because markets were high. Most investors and clients don't understand that concept because it doesn't feel safe, and they're afraid of making a mistake.

It's easy to say, "This could be the wrong time. Why don't I just wait and see?" The illusion of timing the market perfectly is a myth, though. When we get client deposits at my firm, Pacific Capital, we survey their investment needs based on what they own and what their goals are. Then we fully invest the funds. We don't wait.

Sometimes people ask me if I freak out when the markets have a sharp downturn. Well, no. I check the markets every once in a while, and if they're down, it's often a good time to buy some investments at a discounted price. What a novel concept! Everyone talks about buying low, selling high, but almost no one does it. As an investor, you don't benefit from "dusty money," that is, money sitting on the sidelines and doing nothing but waiting. That's wasting the investment opportunity.

The same can happen to your time. If you spend that precious resource on distractions like scrolling through social media and news every day, you'll never get back the compound interest you could have earned by investing that time more wisely.

Capital in motion wins.

Chad and Tony Robbins at their
Zenith Private Business Club Mastermind

As my friend Tony Robbins always says, "progress equals happiness." The opposite of that is getting caught in paralysis by analysis. There's a steep cost to fear and hesitation. You could spend your whole life anticipating and being fearful about what might happen, or you can go for it.

Though I own a wealth management business, I'm not going to discuss what to do with your money. In this book, I'm talking about what to do with your *life*.

Whatever you spend the most time and focus on is what you're invested in. We're all invested in something, whether we intentionally chose it or just stumbled into it. So choose wisely. What and how much you invest in today will shape how you live ten years from now. You may not consciously realize all the consequences of your investments today, but they'll show up in the future.

> *We're all invested in something, whether we intentionally chose it or just stumbled into it. Choose wisely.*

In almost every case, if you're thinking about doing something good, it's better to do it now.

I knew a couple who had scrimped and saved their entire life for retirement and planned a two-month vacation around the world.

They'd been talking about this dream trip and adjusting the future itinerary year after year. As soon as they reached their sixties, the wife became terminally ill and died within six months of their retirement. As a result, the couple never took that trip and never did all the things they planned to do together.

That happened in early 2004; I was just twenty-five years old and young in my career. Their sad circumstances left a strong impression on me. The husband came and sat at our conference room table to discuss his retirement and wept. He couldn't believe they'd waited so long to do all the things they'd talked about doing "someday in the future," and now that day would never come. It was so painful and sad to see. I can still picture his face, full of regret and sadness.

When you realize what's truly at stake, it shapes how you treat your time here and what you're willing to delay. I don't suggest you go out and blow all your money irresponsibly because "YOLO," and you *do* need to plan for the future. But I would also never say to invest 100 percent of your income for the future and live like a miser. Fortunately, there's a middle path where you can invest, be financially responsible, and prepare for your future, while also living a good life right now.

The world tells you to build your career before you create your family, that it's no longer a good idea to get married young, that kids are too expensive, and that it's too hard to run a business while parenting young kids. To further that point, the average age of marriage (men/women) in the U.S. has moved from 22/20 to 31/29, and the media touts the cost of raising a child to be north of $400,000. The conventional wisdom advises you to succeed financially and buy your first home before even thinking of starting a family.

My wife and I decided to say no to the conventional wisdom. We married young and became parents young, and I know what you might be thinking: having five kids in California is crazy! But I wouldn't have it any other way.

Amber, Beckham, Sterling, McKinley, Pierce, Chad, and Bentley

I made a conscious decision to put my family first. I was fortunate to have friendships with incredibly successful friends who were twenty years ahead of me. They had the wealth and freedom, but they also carried deep regret for sacrificing their families to get it. As much success as they had, I knew I never wanted to make that trade.

I chose to never lose sight of my why. My family is my why—and they deserve my full presence. Could I have been twice as wealthy financially? Maybe. But I'm 10X wealthier in life because I have no regrets—and my wife and kids think I'm the best husband and father they could ever ask for. That's real wealth.

−CHRIS JOHNSON,
  FOUNDER AND CEO, PASSIVE CANDIDATE PRO

THE LEGACY OF FULL INVESTMENT

Craig and Betsy Willardson, Chad's parents

My parents are an excellent example of living a Fully Invested life. They didn't delay starting their family and didn't chase success to the point of sacrificing their family life. They've kept family commitments at the center of their life since the day they married, back in May 1977. Sadly, my mom was diagnosed with a rare form of Parkinson's at age sixty-one, which has slowed her down over the past eight years. My dad has cared for her (almost full-time) and has really shown us kids and grandkids what it means to love your spouse unconditionally. I've always been very close to my parents, who've set an example that I'm striving to follow.

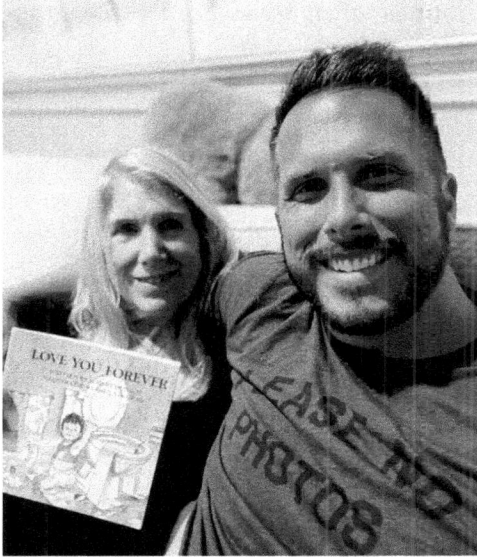

Betsy Willardson (Mom) and Chad, 2025

My mom was extremely invested in us kids. She earned a business degree in marketing but decided to be a full-time stay-at-home mom once we were born. I'm the oldest child with three younger sisters. Crazy story: she almost died while she was eight months pregnant with me, so I was delivered prematurely via an emergency C-section. My parents, both from Orange County, California, were college students at BYU in Utah at the time. The doctor was concerned and told my dad, "This surgery is going to be very risky. You may have to choose who's going to live—your wife Betsy or your baby boy Chad."

My dad felt stressed and panicked and called my grandpa (his father), who was an OB in Beverly Hills, CA. Grandpa, in turn, called the doctor in Provo, Utah, and suggested some different experimental surgery. I don't want to spoil anything for you, but we both made it!

I was just five pounds when I was born and a month premature. I experienced multiple complications at birth. My dad said I looked so tiny he didn't think I had a great chance of surviving, but their doctor said, "Just looking at this baby, I think he's going to be six-foot-five." That's exactly how tall I am today! See how things work out?

Mom had three more kids (all girls) and remained Fully Invested in all of our lives. She volunteered at our schools and went to all our sporting events. She was my Cub Scout leader and my sisters' Girl Scout leader and Sunday School teacher at church. She taught my sisters how to play the piano. She was basically everywhere all the time, doing whatever we needed. One of her legacies will be having shown me the importance of going all in and giving 100 percent effort in every commitment we make, which is something I'm also instilling in my children.

Craig and Betsy with their four kids: Chad, Brittany, Heather, and Brooke

My dad was also Fully Invested. He kept every stat of mine during my games, sitting in the bleachers with his notebook planner and pen, even after a long day of work meetings. What's cool is that he still does this today with my own five kids, who are all athletes. My kids love seeing Grandpa Willie in the bleachers, knowing he's Fully Invested in their success. When I was a baseball pitcher in middle school, he'd play catcher in the backyard and catch all my fastballs in his catcher's mitt, purchased just to help me get reps at home. He'd rebound the basketball as I shot endless free throws, three pointers, and imaginary game-winners! I have so many examples of one of my parents investing in us and giving 100 percent to their faith, family, and professional success—and I saw firsthand the sacrifices and joy that came with it. And now, most of my weekends are spent in bleachers all across the country, cheering for and recording my kids' sports games. I love it, and I'm proud to follow my parents' examples.

Craig (Chad's dad) and Chad, early 1980s in Orange County, California

Early in my career, when my children were very young, I chose to devote all the energy and time I could into the large, prestigious CPA firm I worked for in Los Angeles. Late nights, weekends, and holidays were commonly part of my work routine; I wanted to follow the example of senior firm members and build a career reputation that would lead to a partnership. Ultimately, I thought long-term success and compensation would benefit my family, even while I was absent too often.

After a few years on that treadmill and observing firsthand the common burnout of more senior firm executives, I knew the core family values that I inherently believed in would not be possible in that environment. I needed more investment and involvement in that which I treasured most—my family. I left the world of public accounting and accepted positions in the private business world where I could manage my time more realistically. My goal was to focus on family with a clear head while still progressing at work in a corporate environment that I enjoyed and controlled to a greater degree."

−CRAIG WILLARDSON,
  RETIRED FOOD INDUSTRY CEO AND CHAD'S DAD

WHAT TO EXPECT IN THIS BOOK

Here's a fun story for you: Do you remember the famous singer Brian McKnight (19-time Grammy-nominated musician), whose love songs topped the charts in the nineties and early 2000s? He basically wrote and sang all the love songs the DJs played at dances for more than a decade of my youth! Brian approached me recently at a business mastermind in Arizona and told me that while he admired my success and business growth, he followed my posts on social media not because of business success, but because of my dedicated approach to family life. He interviewed me for his social media segment on fatherhood, and we had a great conversation. Here's what Brian McKnight said about it:

> I requested to interview Chad because I consider him the authority on being successful in business *and* in his family life. I don't take most people at face value; I watch them and see what they're really about, and Chad, by the world's standards, has everything a man could possibly want. But he is something more than the businesses he's built and the books he's written. I've seen it with my own eyes; he's completely invested in his marriage and family. And in my mind, *that's* what makes him truly legendary and someone to be admired.

Brian McKnight and Leilani McKnight, Amber and Chad

Am I telling you this to pat myself on the back? No! (But it's a cool story, right? Brian McKnight! Come on.) My point is that when you live your life Fully Invested, people recognize that, especially when you're authentic about it.

People who follow me on LinkedIn often say I have too much going on. They ask, "How do you do all this? How do you have multiple businesses and still go to your kids' games? From the outside, it looks overwhelming and stressful." I can see that. I've learned to be very intentional with my time and energy in order to really live this way.

I've distilled it into seven **Fully Invested Frameworks**[IP] to maximize my time at work and with family, and I'm sharing them with you in this book so you can achieve the same results in your life. Here they are:

1. Expand your vision to elevate your future.[IP]
2. Master the all-in mindset.
3. Get great at saying no.
4. Activate strengths to amplify success.[IP]
5. Lead with the power of presence.
6. Build championship teams.
7. Choose your people to choose your path.

Besides the frameworks, you'll also find an implementation challenge at the end of each chapter. I encourage you to take these challenges on and not to let excuses or procrastination get in the way. You (and your family) will be blown away by the results!

By applying these Fully Invested Frameworks, you can focus on your legacy, knowing you have Fully Invested your energy in living the best life possible—with the deepest connections to the people who matter most.

I feel such a healthy sense of urgency because I've seen people around me unexpectedly die. Sounds harsh, but it's true. I'm sure you have too. And it happens more often when we reach a certain age. The worst feeling I can imagine is the pain of regret, realizing too late that you were only half-in on this one life you get. Nothing would hurt more than looking back, knowing we missed the mark.

Chad, Sterling, and Pierce, rafting an 18-foot waterfall drop in New Zealand, 2024.

I've committed to living a Fully Invested life, to unleash all potential in my businesses and family. If my life ends sooner than planned, I want the record clear: I never coasted—I went full throttle in every area.

Seriously. You only get one shot at life. My family and I try to experience as much of life as possible, all over the world. As I'm editing this right now, I'm away in South Carolina at my son's basketball tournament while my wife and three of our kids are in Belgium and the Netherlands, and our oldest daughter is serving as a volunteer missionary in Missouri. This is just how we choose to live. Maximizing every day. When the options are to hesitate, take a half-step, or dive in, I dive in—every time. Time is the one asset I can't replenish, and the most valuable day is always the one in front of me.

Speaking of time, I won't waste yours—and you shouldn't waste it either.

So we'll start fast. In chapter 1, you'll do a quick gut-check and score how Fully Invested you are in the big life categories we track inside our ELEVATED community: marriage, family, business/career, health, faith, personal growth, fun and adventure, and finances. I've seen every mix out there: entrepreneurs crushing revenue but running on fumes at home, fitness fanatics with stalled careers, faith-strong leaders whose health is on the back burner, or who are struggling to make ends meet.

Wherever you land, own it. You can't fix what you refuse to see. As my friend Dan Sullivan says, "All progress starts by telling the truth."

Mark your baseline, then let's get to work.

CHAPTER 1

Before We Begin:
Rank and Rate Your Big 8

Once, when I was about five years old, I was playing with a basketball (indoors, where I wasn't *supposed* to be playing basketball) at my grandparents' new beach house. I knocked over a big pitcher of red punch, and it spilled all over their brand-new, bright white couch.

I was mortified. I hid in the corner in shame, knowing I was busted. I figured I was going to be in time out probably for days. Maybe even grounded from the beach. Wrath was coming my way, and the guilt and fear swept over my little heart. I vividly remember what happened next: my grandma Beth came over, knelt down, put her arm around me, and said, "Chad, was that an accident?"

"Yes," I said, hanging my head. "I'm sorry, Grandma."

"Dear, it's okay," she said. "We can fix it. Nothing to worry about. People are more important than things."

It's been more than forty years since that moment. My dear Grandma Beth has long since passed, and I've never forgotten her words.

What my grandma did that day—besides being who she always was, a wonderful and loving person—is a lesson on priorities. We would be wise to take that same lesson from Grandma Beth.

Grandma Beth and Chad, early 1980s, at Grandma's house

People are more important than things, definitely. That was true when I was five and is still true for me today. And my priorities as an adult reflect that by keeping this order: God, my wife Amber, our five children, and my extended family and friends. After getting *your* order straightened out, you still have a lot of priorities and decisions to make. Your life has different seasons, and what matters most today may not be your top priority in fifteen years. Your list can shift order.

In our ELEVATED coaching community, we group life categories into the Big 8:

1. Health and Wellness
2. Key Relationships
3. Money and Wealth
4. Family
5. Faith and Spirituality
6. Personal Growth
7. Business
8. Fun and Adventure

FULLY INVESTED LIFE ASSESSMENT ™

ELEVATED
FULLY INVESTED

Assess where you're thriving and where you need to ELEVATE

Date _____

RANK
Your Prioritization
1-8

1 — Health & Wellness
2 — Key Relationships
3 — Money & Wealth
4 — Family
5 — Faith & Spirituality
6 — Personal Growth
7 — Business
8 — Fun & Adventure

RATE
Yourself In Each
1-10

Health & Wellness   Key Relationships   Money & Wealth   Family

Faith & Spirituality   Personal Growth   Business   Fun & Adventure

30

For a downloadable worksheet and more resources, scan this QR code:

Before we get to the Fully Invested Frameworks and how to live all-in both at work and at home, we need to get real for a minute. Take a look at the Big 8 one more time. Today, maybe personal growth ranks higher than finances. Or maybe getting in excellent shape and prioritizing your health is your number one focus right now. There's no wrong answer. You decide.

Do a three-minute exercise for me: Get out a piece of paper (or the Notes app on your phone) and rank the Big 8 for yourself. Rank them 1–8. Which is most important to you? Least? Take your time with them and order them honestly. Trust me, taking a couple of minutes to do this now will make this book 10x more impactful for you personally.

Once you've completed your ranked list, rate yourself on a scale of one to ten (one being the lowest, ten being the highest) in terms of how well you think you're doing right now. If health and wellness are important to you (number two on your list, for example) but you rarely make time for them, you might give yourself a three or four in that area. Be brutally honest. This is the time to assess how close you are to the life you truly want, and to see where you need to assign more or less energy and attention.

Ranking and rating your Big 8 will help you get so much more out of this book because you'll naturally see which of the Fully Invested Frameworks you should start implementing first based on the areas where you need the most help. In a way, these frameworks are the paths to the life you want, the solutions to the low ratings for your highly ranked priorities. (Remember: being Fully Invested in your family doesn't mean your business goals suffer or that you lose your edge. It ensures that the time you devote to your business is fully optimized because you're operating from a place of genuine support and fulfillment.)

I know you might be thinking, *I don't need to do this exercise. I already know what's important to me and where my strengths and deficits are, so I'll skip over this part and keep reading.*

If that's you, pump the brakes now! The impact of what I'm sharing here is only as valuable as the effort you give, and if you're reading a book called "Fully Invested" and you're not Fully Invested in the main exercise, you won't get what you want out of this book. Plus, when you pause for a few minutes to reflect on your Big 8, your answers might surprise you! I've seen it happen again and again in our ELEVATED community.

*ELEVATED Members at our Mastermind In-Person Event,
Dana Point, California, 2024*

So please take this seriously. And once you've got your ranking and ratings, keep them top of mind as you read the rest of this book. Your future self will thank you.

And with that, let's get started.

CHAPTER 2

Expand Your Vision, Elevate Your Future

As Proverbs 29:18 says, "Without vision, the people perish."

If you don't have a vision, where are you even going? Think about it. Your destination has to be clear before you can take off. A jet at full throttle without a flight plan just burns fuel and circles the sky; vision and a clear destination turn that speed into purpose by taking you where you want to go. We've never taken off in the plane without first knowing exactly where we want to land. Sticking with the plane analogy, you need to make sure the people on board your plane also want to go to the same destination. Would they even get on the plane if they didn't know where you—and they—are headed? If your vision isn't clear (or big enough), people don't want to be a part of it.

Jonny Baird, Craig Willardson, Danny Holmoe, Tyler Haws, Brandt Adams, Casey Adams, Chad Lewis, Chad Willardson, and Randy Francis

Your view of the future needs to be clear and expansive enough to include others' goals, so that the important people in your life are also excited about the destination. That means that they can see themselves achieving their own dreams by joining you. Otherwise, they'll find a different plane with a distinct destination and join someone else's journey.

The same happens within families. If people don't feel excited by family life and like how they can grow and evolve within it, they'll look for outside groups and other sources of fulfillment. If nobody in your family knows what you stand for or where you're headed, how can they be excited about the journey together? As a leader, it's your role to provide that clear vision and help them see where you're headed, and to inspire and support everyone in your family on the way there.

Your success as a visionary leader flows from having a big enough vision to confidently say that everyone you live and work with can grow, succeed, and thrive within your vision. Part of your job as a Fully Invested leader[IP] is to get people excited about the big goal and show them how important they are to reaching it! How will stretching for your big goal help *them* thrive and succeed?

If your team doesn't feel ownership over the mission, they won't be Fully Invested. Sadly, that's how most people feel. A recent Gallup study found that 85 percent of people are unhappy in their jobs, with 60 percent being emotionally detached and 19 percent being miserable. Only 15 percent of workers are actively engaged in their work.[1] People never go all-in for a company—but they *do* go all-in for a mission that excites them.

Instead of just stating your vision, ask:

How do you see your role shaping the future of this company?

What excites you most about what we're building?

What would make you proud to say, 'I helped make this happen'?

These questions encourage your team members to move from being renters to owners. They stop seeing their job as a paycheck and start seeing it as a purpose.

Remember, creating this big tent doesn't mean bending your vision to their opinions or diluting it with outside voices. Be sure to make it clear and broad enough so that there's room for everyone to grow and expand.

ELEVATED Team, 2024

Neliza Becker, Caitlin Nierenberg, Oriya Hirschhorn, Lindsey Fisher, Kirsten Jones, Esty Angel, Natasha Schiffman, Jenessa Catterson, Trav Bell, Amber Willardson, and Chad

BIG VISION AT PACIFIC CAPITAL

Pacific Capital HQ Ribbon Cutting event: Morgan Fippinger, Randy Francis, Aurielle West, Josh Cognilio, Chad, Amber, Oriya Hirschhorn, Katrina Samuel, Neliza Berka, and Cori Parks

I've put this principle into practice at Pacific Capital by giving people specific roles that match each team member's talents and interests. We assign specialty job functions based on employees' natural superpowers—what they're great at and what they actually love to do. We're not obsessed with job titles. Instead, we focus on what they can contribute that helps clients succeed and simultaneously gives them energy at work.

Everyone who works at Pacific Capital knows there's not a list of titles or length of tenure where they automatically get a raise or rise to the next position. Instead, there's an individual career path for each person based on how they can expand, grow, and evolve their skills and the value they bring to the business and our clients.

As team members help the firm grow by serving our clients better, they also individually earn more money and take on more responsibilities. As they grow and expand their expertise, they become more valuable to our clients, and our business continues to grow. It's exciting to watch them grow in the areas that get them excited about their work. Personal and professional growth in that setting are intertwined.

What about your clients and customers? Remember, clients hire you and your company once *they* feel understood and see that you can help them get what *they* want. If you can tap into your client's vision and help them articulate and clarify it, then you can show them a path to get from where they are to where they want to be. Make sure you're tapping into *their* vision. Dig deep into what *they* want. You should not be trying to get your clients to fit into *your* vision. That's backwards. Instead, show them what you offer that helps them achieve their vision, and you'll never run out of business.

> *If you can tap into your client's vision and help them articulate and clarify it, then you can show them a path to get from where they are to where they want to be.*

FAMILY VISION

To incorporate vision into my home life, my wife and I do a vision board activity with our kids during the last week of every year. Our family vision board time is a special occasion, and we really enjoy looking back and seeing pictures of previous years and vision boards together.

As a family, we get magazines, scissors, tape, newspapers, stickers, poster boards, markers, and crayons. Each person makes their own vision board, and we also create one as a family. We keep it simple with four quadrants (categories for our goals)—spiritual, physical, intellectual, and social—but you can adapt this exercise to use whatever lenses work for your situation.

We write specific goals and include corresponding pictures or stickers that visually represent our vision. For example, if one of my goals is to get physically fit, then I'll include pictures of someone lifting weights or playing sports along with pictures of healthy food. My specific written goal might say, "Exercise one hour per day, six days a week." The pictures will help me visualize that concrete plan.

We want the kids to set at least one or two highly specific, measurable goals in each of the four categories. This applies whether they're three years old or eighteen. The goals will evolve as they mature. Then we place the vision boards where everyone can see them.

For the family vision board, we focus on shared experiences—things that we want to do and learn together. Maybe we want to try something brand new, like going river rafting. Maybe we want to learn a new skill together or start a new family business. Each member of the family has a voice and contributes their input so that we all feel invested in the plan for the coming year.

Beckham, Pierce, McKinley, Chad, Sterling, and Bentley

Pierce, McKinley, Sterling, Chad, Amber, Beckham, and Bentley

Pierce, Chad, Sterling, Amber, Bentley, and Beckham

As the school year ends, our family sits down and creates individual bucket lists that kick off when the summer begins. Our girls, especially, enjoy decorating their posters with markers and colored paper. They hang their bucket lists in their rooms and make it a habit of crossing off each goal with a large check mark. We make it a frequent topic of conversation to keep the vision in front of us. The entire experience creates a fun and unifying activity for the whole family.

**–KARY OBERBRUNNER,
CEO OF IGNITING SOULS AND INSTANT IP**

WHAT TO DO WHEN YOU DON'T HAVE TIME

I know what you're thinking: *I don't have time for this, and I don't even know if my kids would be into this.* Maybe you don't have time to sit down and do vision boards with your family because you've already got five hundred other things on your to-do list. And that's the entire point. You actually don't have time *NOT* to do this. What's more important than setting up a great vision for the future of your life and your family's life?

When people tell me they're too busy to join our growth mastermind program, ELEVATED, I say, "That's exactly why you should be in ELEVATED. We help you free up time to focus more on what matters most." When you say you're too busy, that's exactly the signal you need to try a new approach.

I had my doubts about whether my family would agree to creating vision boards a decade ago, yet it's now something we all look forward to. It's part of who we are. Because of this process, my kids have achieved incredible things. As a twelve-year-old seventh grader, our daughter McKinley had a picture of a college basketball player and then a little sticker from BYU. At that age, she was very much a beginner in the sport. On her vision board, she set specific goals to help measure her extra practice and improve her skills. I was helping her learn how to shoot baskets in the backyard. Back then, she struggled to dribble the ball between her legs—but that ambitious goal was on her vision board. Fast-forward to the week of her high school graduation, and BYU offered her a spot on the basketball team. Just reflecting on it feels awesome as her dad: McKinley set specific goals and was Fully Invested in the big vision of her future. And seven years later, she put on the jersey to play Division 1 basketball at BYU in the Big 12 Conference! This stuff really works!

McKinley's hoop dreams realized, and her proud dad, Chad

Would our family achieve big goals without these vision boards and planning sessions each year? I don't think so. Having a vision board with your most important goals clearly stated gives you a daily visual reminder of where you want to invest your time. And no, it's not a one-and-done activity. Every time you look at it, you have the opportunity to advance yourself—and your family and career—a little bit further. And if you're half-committed to your own goals and ignore these frameworks, you just might miss out on your own potential for a bigger and better future.

MISSION STATEMENTS FROM A FAMILY PERSPECTIVE

Almost any strategy that's successful in your business world can be adapted and applied to your family life. You'd never run a business without a mission statement, business plan, and shared core values. So why would you try to run a successful family without these elements in place?

My friend Mark Timm wrote a book about treating family like a corporation, where everyone's a board member and a shareholder. He says he's the CEO of the world's most valuable business: his family. He positions himself as helping leaders leverage their business success to win at home.

A strong family mission will stay steady (like an anchor) despite the changing pressures of the world, and your vision can evolve as you learn and grow and as conditions change. Your mission gives you a North star, but you also need to be agile, just as you would in business. If someone gets sick, you need to move out of state, or other circumstances shift what makes sense for your vision, then you need that combination of guidance from your core values with the freedom to adjust.

Your foundation's strength gives you the ability to be agile with the individual decisions you need to make. You want to build on stone, not sand, because without that strong foundation, every storm risks crumbling what you've built. Like the song says, "the wise man built his house upon a rock."[2] You can't grow as a family unit without a strong foundation.

GOAL-SETTING AS A FAMILY

Marriage is like a business partnership, with co-CEOs. We each have our own goals, and then we have our goals as a family, which we revise and reinforce at the end of each year. We also have personal stretch goals.

Chad and Amber, Pacific Capital HQ in Corona, California

My wife and I have attended many entrepreneurial couples' retreats, which offer a great chance for us to spend time away from home without the kids and connect on a different level. That might seem like an unconventional priority for someone talking about Fully Investing in family, but a strong marriage is essential to going all in at home. Many of my friends will not spend time away without the kids, but I think it's extremely healthy for couples to travel alone, reconnect, talk about life, and strengthen their connection. If you have kids, you and your spouse were together before the kids arrived, and you'll be there after they've grown and left the house. The best time to water that relationship garden was yesterday, but the second-best time is now.

When my wife and I travel alone, it gives us a chance to talk about what matters to us, what we're struggling with, how we can better support each other, and what we're excited about together. We talk about big ideas and set goals together. At the entrepreneurial marriage retreats, we've had the chance to talk about how to deal with the stress of entrepreneurship as a couple because running a business tends to put more pressure on families and marriages than having a regular nine-to-five job. There's inherently more risk and uncertainty.

Chad and Amber, Iceland

Amber and Chad in Dubai, 2024

I also carve out time to spend with each of my kids individually, away from home. Many of these trips are out-of-state sports tournaments where it's me alone with one of them. The time on the flights, in the hotels, before and after games is precious, undivided one-on-one time with each of them. It's year 10 and counting of travel sports, where I've had these opportunities and created memories with each kid.

If you think about it, what's more important than finding more ways to leverage your time to connect with the people you love? Commit today to being more intentional about how you spend your time. An hour lost to doom-scrolling on social media or news apps is an hour you could have spent deepening the relationship with your spouse or child.

An hour lost to doom-scrolling on social media or news apps is an hour you could have spent deepening the relationship with your spouse or child.

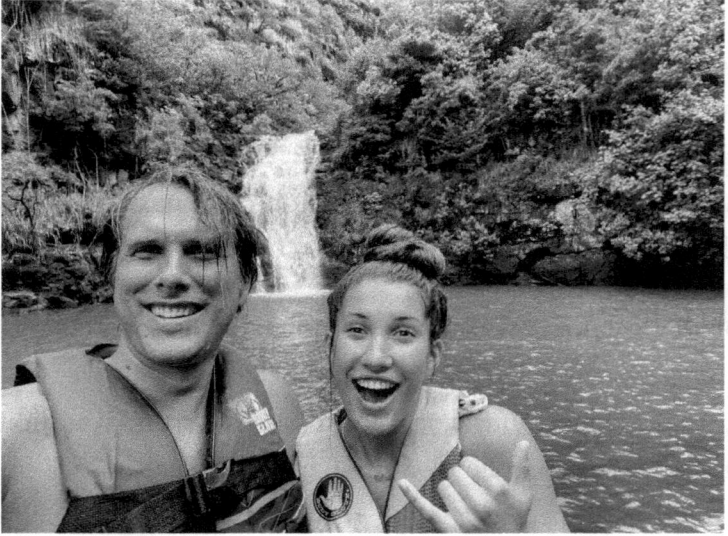

Chad and McKinley, Oahu, Hawaii, 2023

Pierce and Chad, Oahu, Hawaii 2025

Sterling and Chad at the Lakers game, 2024

Bentley and Chad in Nevada for her volleyball tourney, 2025

Chad and Beckham in Spain, 2024

In our family, we approach vision casting and goal setting with the same intentionality we'd bring to running a business—because our family is our most important team. My husband and I see ourselves as the leadership team for our home, so it starts with us getting aligned first. Each quarter, we carve out time together to reflect on how the last quarter went and set clear priorities for the quarter ahead. We check everything we're doing—both the goals and the pace— against two critical anchors: our "No Matter What ™" Family Values and our Family Decade Dream ™.

Our Family Decade Dream is a shared ten-year vision that articulates what we want our family to look and feel like a decade from now—what memories we'll have made, what habits we'll have built, how we'll be showing up for each other, and what kind of legacy we're creating together. To get to that vision, we use a guided exercise that asks us to imagine our lives ten years from now in vivid detail—then we reverse-engineer what needs to happen now to make that dream a reality. This long-term vision becomes our filter. It helps us cut through the noise of outside expectations and pressures and stay focused on what truly matters to us.

From there, we break the vision into quarterly priorities and use weekly Family Alignment Meetings™ to check in on progress. My husband and I meet each week to review upcoming logistics, clarify who's owning what, and ensure we're both moving the needle on our shared goals. It creates an open channel for real-time adjustments and prevents things from falling through the cracks.

—ANN C. SHEU,
FOUNDER & CEO, MPOWERED FAMILIES

THE GOLD OF STRETCH GOALS

Stretch goals are key to being a Fully Invested leader. You're not out to live a "regular" or "mediocre" life, so why set "regular" goals? Here's how this can look: at Pacific Capital, I set an ambitious goal of attracting more than $200 million of new investment deposits and only five new clients (higher value clients as our focus) as a team in 2024. I'm not sure everyone on the team initially believed it was possible, but we ended up achieving it *before* the end of Q3! A huge success for our team.

To celebrate, I decided that instead of doing our typical Christmas dinner party in Newport Beach, we would take the entire company and their spouses on a five-day couples' 5-star retreat to Cabo to celebrate. I made this announcement in Q3 at a family swim barbecue party with all the team members and their families. The wife of one team member told me, "I remember when you set that goal in January. My husband came home and said, 'Chad set another ridiculous goal, and we probably have no chance of reaching it, but we'll see.'"

Pacific Capital Team and Spouses in Cabo San Lucas, 2024

I laughed out loud when I heard that story, because in the end, we didn't even need the whole year to meet the goal! Moving forward, he'll understand that we can do big things here and that no goals are impossible.

At the time of this writing, our stretch goal for our ELEVATED community is to finish our customized community app and welcome five hundred additional new members by the end of 2025 (we have just under one hundred members now). It would make more sense to set a goal for 20 percent growth or even a 2X jump, but that's not exciting enough for me.

Ask yourself: What could you accomplish if you Fully Invested in your stretch goals? The results might surprise you. If this idea feels uncomfortable to you, that's normal. Most people set goals that are too small and uninspiring because that's what they see others doing, and it feels safer. It's important to know how to reverse that impulse. We make thinking ambitiously a cornerstone of ELEVATED, and our members talk about how they begin thinking way bigger within the first two months of joining.

From school to corporate environments, most people are taught to be "realistic" rather than ambitious. I think you need to take the opposite approach: be ambitious and maximize leverage.

If you read my fourth book, *Fit for Wealth*, you might remember how I made my own version of "S.M.A.R.T. goals" and replaced "realistic" with "ridiculous" for the R. You won't achieve your real potential by settling for "realistic" goals anyway. An awareness of leverage goes back to delegation. People who think small believe *they* need to be the ones to do everything *themselves*. Part of our goal at ELEVATED is to surround high achievers with other high achievers to amplify their visions of freedom and success. When you're surrounded by other people thinking big and pushing the envelope, you're 100 percent more likely to think bigger about what's possible.

I still remember back in 2018, sitting in a mastermind session in Toronto, Canada, when I heard a successful entrepreneur share that he no longer used his email. He said his executive assistant handled his work email inbox, and it had freed up fifteen hours a week for him. That seemed like a crazy goal because I was spending hours every week reading, responding to, and sending emails. But hearing him say it changed my belief. Get yourself around the right people, and you'll believe you can do what previously seemed way out of reach. You'll see other people achieving incredible things and realize if they can do it, so can you. You'll feel supported and get excited about new opportunities, making you more willing to take chances than you would be on your own.

Sometimes you set a stretch goal and fall short. The reason you fell short might be that you weren't Fully Invested (think of your last weight loss or fitness goal). Or you may need to reevaluate how you define failure for yourself. What does failure even mean? If you reach for something ambitious and don't quite get there, you've likely still gone farther than you would have if you'd played it safe and stuck with "realistic" goals.

Why should you keep setting ambitious goals if you might fall short? Falling short or losing some of the time is inevitable. How you respond determines whether you ultimately win big or retreat into mediocrity. High achievers think big and learn to move on from failures quicker. Next time you set a stretch goal and don't quite make it, ask yourself: What did this teach me, and how am I better because of it?

My relationship with delegation has transformed. Early on my journey, I thought I had to do everything myself to maintain quality.

But as I expanded into multiple ventures, I realized that true leadership isn't about being indispensable; it's about building teams that can exceed what you could accomplish alone. Now I delegate not just tasks but entire visions to capable leaders. Because when you delegate with purpose and trust, you're not just freeing up your time; you're multiplying your impact and empowering others to step into their greatness. The evolution has been from "I must do this" to "Who can do this better than me?" That shift has been liberating for everyone involved.

This doesn't just free up my schedule; it creates what I call the prosperity of time.

This prosperity of time isn't just about having more hours in my day; it's about having the mental space to innovate, the emotional bandwidth to mentor the next generation of leaders, and the freedom to pursue ventures that ignite my soul.

When we master delegation, we don't just become more efficient, we become more human. We reclaim the right to think, dream, create, and inspire.

That's the ultimate return on investment that no financial portfolio can match.

–IMAN MUTLAQ,
FOUNDER INGOT BROKERS GROUP

VISION IN MARRIAGE

Amber and I married in 2001 as broke college sophomores and lived in a four-hundred-square-foot basement apartment. I often walked or took the public shuttle bus to work, where I made just $5.25 an hour working at a marketing call center. We were both full-time students and barely getting by financially.

Chad and Amber's wedding pics, San Diego, CA, in 2001

There's no way we could have predicted just how amazing and abundant our lives would be twenty-four years later (saying this with respect, humility, and giving credit to God, not to myself, knowing that financial wealth is not the end-all, be-all). We're so grateful for the family life we get to experience and see how the vision we had as newlyweds has come to pass over time. My wife, Amber, was the fourth of six kids. I was the first of four. We wanted to have a big family with at least four kids, and we dreamed of having the time and resources to give them experiences through travel and adventure. We also wanted to have a faith-based family. We wanted to be active, teach our kids how to serve others, and experience different parts of the world together. We also wanted to be financially responsible. These were all parts of the vision back in our early twenties in that small, one-bedroom apartment.

Some couples never talk about those subjects before marriage, but we took a marriage prep class in college after we got engaged. The professor had us write down our vision and goals together and discuss them. We talked about our hopes and dreams, which helped lay the groundwork for getting and staying aligned in our relationship. As a result, we were aligned on our vision for the family from the beginning.

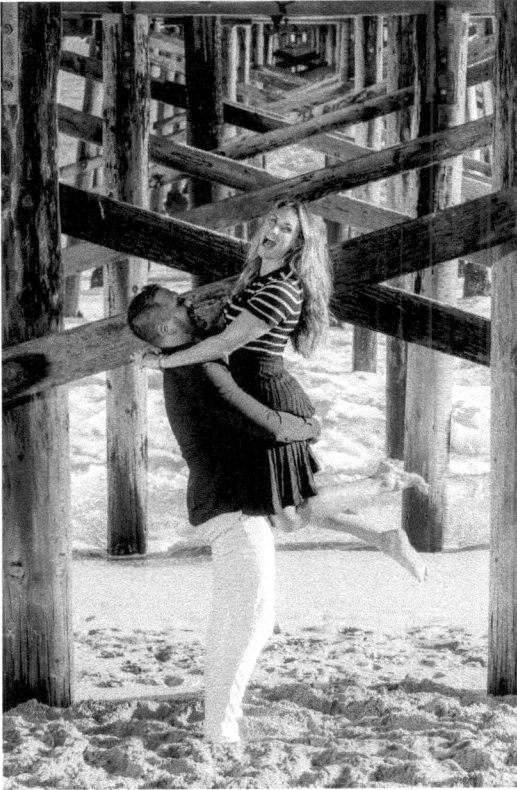

Chad and Amber at Balboa Pier, CA 2025

Our life today is a product of following through on that shared vision. We didn't just luck into it. It didn't happen by accident. And it wasn't a perfect, smooth road either. We've had our struggles and disagreements. We've juggled parenting young kids and babies, experienced the stress of entrepreneurship, and found ways to stay connected through all the chaos. It wasn't always easy. And it's still not easy, but it's so worth it.

Great success doesn't come by chance. It always starts with a clear vision.

Our family has aligned around what we call the "Giant 5 Vision"—our top five priorities:

1. *Faith in God. This comes first. We aim to grow in our faith, both individually and together.*

2. *Strong Marriages (or Preparation for One). For those of us who are married, we prioritize building strong, joyful, Christ-centered marriages. For those not yet married, we focus on preparation—emotionally, spiritually, and relationally.*

3. *Parenting Well. This applies to us as parents, but also to our children, who are learning to honor their father and mother—because the Bible promises in Deuteronomy 6:3 that "it will go well with you" when you do.*

4. *Health and Well-being. Life is an energy game. If we want to bring our best to family, business, and ministry, we have to steward our health.*

5. *Creating Value for Others. We believe in using our God-given gifts to create value through business and ministry. These priorities guide us beyond trends, moods, or career shifts.*

When life feels off-track, we ask a simple question: Where am I right now in my faith, my marriage, my parenting, my health, and my contribution to others? Then we take action to grow in that area.

–CHAD JOHNSON,
THE GIANT 5 GUY™, FATHER OF 11, ENTREPRENEUR, AUTHOR, SPEAKER, COACH

FULLY INVESTED FRAMEWORKS: VISION AND MISSION

GROW

It's important to set a vision that integrates business growth and family priorities with a unified mission. For example, if I'm aiming for business growth, then including strategic hiring and delegation in that plan simultaneously creates more income and more freedom. That growth, in turn, allows me to have a greater impact for our clients while also enjoying more travel experiences with my family and kids. The business goals align with fully investing in my family. There's growth with a purpose. I use this acronym, GROW, to keep this vision top of mind:

- **G**uided by Purpose
- **R**elationships First
- **O**ngoing Growth
- **W**ell-Being and Joy

CHALLENGE: THE FAMILY CEO[IP]

Purpose: Teach kids and spouse to take leadership roles in the family, encouraging them to think proactively about how to improve home life.

Step 1: Ask each family member:

- *If you were the CEO of our family for a day, what's one thing you'd improve?*
- *What's one area we succeed together in our family?*

Step 2: Let everyone share their ideas in a Family Team Meeting.

- Encourage big thinking—this isn't about chores and checklists; it's about creating a better home culture. Ideas could include:
  - More fun traditions or family trips
  - New ways to improve morning or dinner routines
  - A new family standard or expectation to make life smoother

Step 3: Choose one or two ideas and let family members own the implementation.

- Example: If a child suggests "more one-on-one parent-kid outings," let them create the schedule and pick the activities.
- If a spouse suggests a "tech-free dinner night," let them set the rules and make it a success.

Why It Works:

- Shifts family members from passive participants to active contributors.
- Builds leadership, responsibility, and teamwork at home.
- Makes family life feel like a shared mission, not something managed by parents.

KEY TAKEAWAYS

▸ Part of your job as a Fully Invested leader is to get people excited about the big goal and show them how they fit into the long-term vision. How will what you want to achieve help them thrive?

▸ If your team doesn't feel ownership over the mission, they won't be Fully Invested.

▸ When you say you're too busy, that's the signal to try a new approach.

▸ You're not out to live a "regular" life, so why set "regular" goals?

▸ Marriage is like a business partnership (but with way more love), with co-CEOs and an aligned vision.

CHAPTER 3
Master the All-In Mindset

Do you make excuses and call them "reasons?"

If so, you're not alone.

Many busy entrepreneurs make excuses or justify these "reasons" why they can't give their family their full attention. For instance, you've got a big project or need to build your business, and this is just how it's got to be right now. The antidote to this problem is an all-in mindset that extends beyond just your business. Ask yourself, *What would a Fully Invested leader do in my situation?*

An all-in mindset is willing to try and fail. It maintains discipline. It means you do hard things even when you don't feel like it. With an all-in mindset, the Fully Invested leader doesn't procrastinate or ask for handouts—they do the work. When you're all in, you don't hesitate or delay. You don't get trapped in paralysis by analysis or worry about what other people think.

That sounds powerful, right? Let's look at how to do it.

STAYING COMMITTED

We have a big family, and there are times when the kids all have different activities and need to be in different places at the same time. No joke, one Saturday our kids had eleven games in four different cities! It feels like chaos, but I wouldn't have it any other way. Instead of our kids missing their games and commitments, we figure out how to make it happen. That's what being a Fully Invested parent means. You find a way to make it work, even when it's not convenient. *Hint: it's not supposed to be.*

One rule I have is that if one of my kids asks to play something with me, I always say yes. Lately, my youngest son, Beckham, is obsessed with ping-pong. No matter what I'm doing, if he says, "Dad, can you play a game of ping-pong with me?" I always say yes. We now play every single day that we're home. It might only take fifteen to twenty minutes, but it's hugely meaningful time together. He even wrote on my Father's Day card, "I love it when we play ping-pong together." Someday, he'll grow out of wanting to play with me every day. So the time to connect with him is right now, not some imaginary date when I'm "less busy."

Beckham and Chad in the Cayman Islands, 2025

I also prioritize going to my kids' games, award ceremonies, performances, and other activities. At Pacific Capital, we encourage our team members to do the same. This is not just a perk for me as the owner. If there's a ceremony during the school day and they want to see their child get an award, they can leave work to see it and come back to the office later.

THE TRADE-OFF MYTH

Many entrepreneurs have convinced themselves that building a successful business requires a trade-off with family, and that's just part of the deal. I've heard so many people say some version of "Once I hit _____, then I'll have time for my family" or "Once I'm making $X per year, then I'll consider getting married and starting a family." That's not only a false narrative, it's sad. Doing well at work and having a successful family aren't mutually exclusive. I wrote a viral article for *Entrepreneur* magazine on this topic called "Here's Why Hustle Culture Is a Big Lie."[3] Here's a snippet:

> As someone who has worked hard to grow their business, I can attest that it's okay to take a step back from day-to-day operations and focus on the bigger picture. Your time is limited (and valuable), and the work is endless. You've got to recognize there's only so much you can achieve as an entrepreneur and determine what you're best equipped to take on.

The trade-off mindset is a losing bet. Could my company be bigger if I poured every waking minute into it? Probably. But a fatter bottom line isn't a win if it costs you the very things that give life meaning.

*Chad, Pierce, McKinley, Bentley, Amber, and Sterling,
with Bentley and Beckham in front, 5K race in Turtle Bay, Oahu, 2023.*

STAYING COMMITTED WITHOUT LOSING YOURSELF

Make no mistake about it, I've declined plenty of business-related invitations because I refuse to be an absent husband or dad. If money were my only metric, I could pour many more hours into business. But that tradeoff doesn't make sense to me. Instead, I've learned how to squeeze more results out of each hour so the rest of my time stays open for Amber and the kids.

Back at Merrill Lynch, apart from a brief licensing stipend, my pay was straight commission. So I've never earned a salary in my life. Early on, I saw the fork in the road: be present at home and accept way less income, or get creative and generate more value in less time than the competition. I chose the second path.

Leverage, systems, and high-value work formed my playbook. Because I'm not willing to sacrifice the hours reserved for family, health, church, or the moments that matter most. Early on, my colleagues doubted it would work, yet two decades later, we have thriving businesses, twenty-four years of marriage, and five kids who still like hanging out with us. The results speak for themselves. And for that, we are grateful.

The goal isn't to brag about hours worked or how busy you are. The goal is to be Fully Invested and maximize the impact of each hour. Many hustle gurus ignore every other part of life while they chase significance through work. I agree that hard work is essential, but if work is all you do, you haven't really succeeded.

I was in business seven years before we started having children. At that time, I believed I had to choose between building a successful business and being present at home. It was a constant juggling act in determining what was more important any given day—work or family. What flipped that mindset for me was realizing that my career and business could support my role as a mom, not compete with it. I believe strongly in work-life integration. Instead of trying to keep work and home separate, I've embraced the flexibility my career allows to blend them together. This shift has been empowering. It means I can work hard, serve my clients and team, and still be fully present at home—whether cheering from the sidelines at soccer and lacrosse games, carpooling, helping with homework, or just getting the kids fed and to bed. It's not about sacrificing one for the other—it's about being all in on both, creating a life that's full, meaningful, and being true to who I am.

–JEN BORISLOW,
PRESIDENT AND CEO, BORISLOW INSURANCE

FOSTERING AN ALL-IN MINDSET ON YOUR TEAM

On the professional front, how do you create an environment where people are Fully Invested, striving and driven, and cultivating this mindset of contributing to the overall goal? People often tell me they set big goals for their business, but their teams haven't fully bought into the goals and aren't committed to their vision for growth.

I have an answer for them:

- To empower your team, move them from task-doers to decision makers.
- Teach people to think in terms of ROI, efficiency, and long-term growth, not just daily checklists.
- Don't micromanage them. Instead, coach and support them.

My team would tell you I'm the opposite of a micromanaging leader. If you hire people who only produce results when micromanaged, you've got the wrong people. You're better off setting the vision, leading and training, and then letting people work through issues and challenges on the way to getting results. You can check in to give guidance, leadership, and coaching, but don't be the hero jumping in to save the day and put out all the fires. This approach is better long-term for you and your business, allowing for more autonomy and growth. It creates a "no excuses" culture too.

And it's not just about helping your team and business grow. You've got to personally grow, getting better in business and at home as a Fully Invested leader. Getting better means Fully Investing in communication, including listening to any feedback from the people you care about and work with. As an entrepreneur, you may or may not be used to opening yourself up to correction, but a Fully Invested leader does not get caught up in ego or status. When I'm vulnerable online, my social media gets flooded with hateful comments and criticism. It doesn't bother me one bit. In fact, I've made many videos reading hateful comments and responding in a funny way to them. You can't let negative people or naysayers get to you. A Fully Invested leader is more focused on growth and getting it right than on avoiding disapproval and criticism. The only feedback to pay attention to and take seriously is feedback from the people who are Fully Invested in your vision with you.

> *As an entrepreneur, you may or may not be used to opening yourself up to correction, but a Fully Invested leader does not get caught up in ego or status.*

So much is at stake with your family, and sometimes when you ask what they think could be done differently, they'll raise issues you didn't even think about. They'll point out places where you're wrong and can improve. That's okay—the point isn't to always be right, but to be unified in your values and goals in the home. To be Fully Invested at home, you've got to be open to finding a better way of doing things. Stay coachable, even in your own home.

Every great athlete and business person values coaching and training, from all-time greats like Kobe Bryant and Michael Jordan to Tiger Woods and Roger Federer. They all have great coaches, and they're all being corrected and told to make adjustments all the time. Fully Invested family members and business leaders understand that correction is not criticism. It's okay to be corrected and not take it personally. Instead of feeling chastised or attacked, recognize you have the opportunity to do something differently and better.

My kids know that if I correct them (and I often do), I'm not criticizing; I'm trying to help them in the same way a coach would. My son Sterling recently said, "Dad, does everything have to turn into a lesson?" And we had a great chat about why I'm so engaged in teaching them. Because I want them to grow and thrive more than anything, long after I'm gone. And I value that same kind of feedback and lessons for growth for me from family and trusted team members.

LEARNING TO COLLABORATE IN MARRIAGE

My wife and I have very different communication styles and approaches to decision-making. I'm comfortable with uncertainty and risk-taking and being spontaneous, whereas she likes to be overly prepared as early as possible and is more methodical and conservative. One of the challenges we've always had that brings this difference to light is how we approach vacations and travel.

My preference is to be more spontaneous and plan less. For example, to me, it feels like she wants to create a twenty-seven-point agenda for our beach day, and that just kills the entire vibe. I prefer to check it out, see what we can discover, and how the day goes while maintaining flexibility and keeping options open. That approach often gets us some cool surprises that we couldn't have planned in advance. On the other hand, she wants to maximize the vacation time by prioritizing a long list of what she wants to do and see, many months in advance. My approach makes her feel like we're unprepared and probably going to miss out on opportunities. A completely opposite philosophy.

For example, I could say, "Hey, let's go on a trip to Costa Rica in a few weeks!" Though it wouldn't be fully researched and preplanned far in advance, it would be adventurous, and we'd still pack a ton of exciting adventures in because we'd likely find some great local experts to help us curate a unique trip that no travel blogger could've planned out for us.

Pierce, Chad, Amber, Bentley, Sterling, and Beckham hiking in Peru, 2025

I'm the same way about planning big parties. We could invite three hundred people to come over tomorrow night and hang out in our backyard with a DJ, catering, decorations, the whole nine. I'd find people to do what I needed them to do, and it would be fun. It wouldn't worry me at all, but it would make her absolutely crash and burn. If you think like she does, you might even be sweating right now hearing me describe these big spontaneous events. I'm not saying one way is right and the other is wrong—they're just extremely different.

We had a counseling session on this topic with someone who understands both of us. She said to Amber, "It clearly stresses you out a lot when he wants to do things that are a little more spontaneous and exciting and whatever. But how does it usually turn out?"

Amber said, "It always turns out great, but I don't like that feeling leading up to it. I feel anxious and totally unprepared." The coach's feedback to me was that part of Amber's excitement about trips is the anticipation of knowing exactly what she's going to do on vacation. It gives her something to look forward to. If everything is unplanned and up in the air, she doesn't get the enjoyment of anticipation. I honestly hadn't thought of that before.

We reached a good compromise where some days of our trips can be preplanned for her to enjoy anticipating, while also carving out parts that leave room for me to innovate without feeling as if every minute is scheduled (like I'm being dragged through a school field trip). I want to leave some margin for when we get there, so that when we hear a great suggestion from the locals, we can go and try it. And if the weather changes or unexpected crowds turn up, we can improvise, pivot, and make a better plan! Meeting in the middle works for us in this way, and we're both all-in because, at the end of the day, we both have the same goal, which is to have an incredible trip together, whether as a couple or with our whole family. By working through that point of tension, we learned that we have different styles and sources of enjoyment. We found a blend that works for both of us, and it was great advice.

FULLY INVESTED IN FAITH

My two foundational pillars in life are my family and faith in God. A key principle that connects those two pillars is service to others. One of the pivotal periods in my life was in the late nineties when I was a volunteer church missionary in Lithuania, Latvia, Estonia, and Belarus. At no time in my life have I been more Fully Invested in one purpose than as a full-time volunteer missionary for those two years. Explaining it to a business friend recently, I told him to picture being a monk in a monastery for twenty-four months straight. There's no radio, no dating, no entertainment, no sports, no job, no regular social life. It's pure service and worship for two solid years.

Living in the Baltic States and immersing myself in their culture a few short years after the Soviet Union collapsed was a time of great personal development. It was transformational to say the least. No one spoke English, so I became fluent in Lithuanian and conversational in Russian. I knocked on more than fifty thousand doors during my service, much of the time in the bitter freezing cold, trying to meet people, make friends, serve in the community, and teach them about Christianity and family values.

There was no baby pacifier for that experience. I was in the real world. At age nineteen. I was robbed three times. We were harassed by drunks in the streets on a weekly basis. We didn't have cars or bikes, so we walked the cities or took the public buses. They once tried bikes (the year before I got there), because a lot of missionaries in the US use bikes for transportation. Within two weeks in our Eastern European region, though, every single bike had been stolen!

Chad in Eastern Europe

Two to three weeks a year, the pipes didn't work in our old gray Soviet apartment buildings where we lived. During those weeks, there was no hot water, and it was two degrees outside during the bitter cold winter mornings. We just had to deal with it. Sometimes I'd boil a pot at a time and dump it in the bath. Other times, the faucet would shoot out dirty brown water, and there was nothing we could do. During those two challenging years, I learned that when you're not focused on your own problems and you're Fully Invested in helping other people solve their problems, you're a lot happier.

And getting rejected 99.9 percent of the time taught me not to take rejection personally. I learned how to see things from other perspectives and interact with people who were much different from me. The people I talked to lived in a society and culture new to me. They'd only been free from the Soviets for six to seven years when I got there and were struggling with what freedom really meant.

I learned how to collaborate with a variety of team members during this time, too. I was assigned new partner companions every six to eighteen weeks, and each time it was someone I didn't know who often came from a background distinct to my own.

I also learned to sacrifice, having left behind all the comforts of home. Our communication with family and friends back home was extremely limited. For example, I remember when my parents mailed me a Christmas package, and it was finally delivered in March, but with half of the things stolen from it. Many of my friends and I still say that those were the greatest two years of our lives. Looking back, despite how hard it was, we weren't focused on ourselves at all. Because we were Fully Invested, we felt fulfilled.

When you're not focused on your own problems and you're Fully Invested in helping other people solve their problems, you're a lot happier.

As I write this, my oldest daughter is currently gone on her own volunteer service mission. We dropped her off in Mexico City last year (she's now in Kansas City, Missouri), said goodbye, and haven't seen her in sixteen months. The commitment of being Fully Invested in serving others is part of our family core values and stems from our faith background going back many generations.

McKinley and her missionary companion, Independence, Missouri, 2025

CHOOSING TO SERVE

A mission isn't required in our church, and I'd never force my kids into it. Without their own conviction, they wouldn't enjoy it or even last until the end. That's why watching my daughter thrive out there means so much to me. She's serving strangers, learning Spanish, waking up early, and smiling through the long days because she's Fully Invested in her service.

Before deciding to leave on her mission, she reached her dream goal and played her freshman year of basketball at BYU. With several teammates graduating or transferring, her sophomore year promised more opportunities for playing time on the court. She weighed that opportunity against an eighteen-month church mission and chose the mission. She knows the grind that lies ahead when she returns—getting back into game shape, fighting for her spot—but her faith in God and desire to serve outranked playing time or advancing her basketball career.

I've always been honest with my kids about the sacrifice. A full-time mission isn't a gap-year vacation. You don't get to pick the location. You submit your name and application, and the call comes. If you didn't know already, missionaries pay their own way and work long hours, six-and-a-half days per week. The only way that kind of sacrifice makes sense is if you are all in. Half-in will break you. That principle holds everywhere else in life too: the things that matter most demand your full commitment.

My faith drives everything I do and how I live my life. My purpose is not about me. It's about how I can impact others in a positive way. I want to spend my time making an eternal impact, knowing love is what lasts forever. When thinking about books I want to write or projects I want to invest time and money in, I ask myself, "Will this impact people's souls?" That will determine if I want to do it. I also know I'm here to develop positive leaders who make an impact to create a more positive world, and that drives me and my team.

–JON GORDON,
18X BESTSELLING AUTHOR OF THE ENERGY BUS

WORTHWHILE SACRIFICES

Committing to your family isn't easy either. As the famous speech by Rocky Balboa reminds us, "The world ain't all sunshine and rainbows." Family life brings just as many struggles as in your business career, if not more. However, a Fully Invested leader is more focused on the mission than the cost of getting there.

You'll sacrifice plenty, but if you stay driven by your mission, you won't sacrifice what matters most for what you want today. You'll instead sacrifice the stuff that matters least—your time wasters, vices, and addictions. You'll also maximize your ability to delegate, so that work keeps happening even when you're not the one doing it.

These days, I don't aimlessly wander the Internet or binge-watch news, TV, movies, or any streaming services. And fortunately, I've never "been out drinking with the boys." If I chose to indulge in those behaviors, there'd be no room for me to be Fully Invested in my family and my business growth. My life would be full of excuses and justifications of why I'm not where I could be. Maybe you agree with me; I'd rather decline low-frequency behaviors and distractions and focus on priorities that matter most to me and my family. Better to sacrifice those types of dopamine hits than to be the husband or the dad who looks in the eyes of his family members and says, "Sorry, but I have a meeting."

Yes, I sometimes bring work home, as most hard drivers and achievers do. But I draw boundaries and set aside time to spend with my wife, Janet, and our two sons when they are home. And when we're together, we're TOGETHER, all in, phones down, and fully engaged, present, intentional, and immersed in the moment. That also means we bring our BEST SELF.

Lead from the front. Lead with clarity. Lead with positivity and elevate everyone around you.

Life is way too short, and the clock is spinning fast on all of us. I want to make sure that I'm doing everything I can to dominate every moment that I have left on this planet. And that starts with being fully present, with clear eyes and a full heart for those who matter most to me—family, friends, and business associates. It comes down to a choice—a choice to be more intentional and focused in those moments that matter most.

**–JIM ROME,
MEMBER OF THE RADIO HALL OF FAME AND KEYNOTE SPEAKER**

FULLY INVESTED FRAMEWORKS: AN ALL-IN MINDSET

FAMILY COUNCIL

You have at least one weekly (our Pacific Capital team huddles up *daily* at 8:00 a.m.) group meeting at work—why not at home? How can you expect to avoid communication issues if you literally have zero schedule of home communication? We hold weekly family meetings on Sunday afternoons called a "family council." I remember my parents holding this weekly family session in our family room growing up, and it's a great framework for staying aligned and unified as a family.

Rotate who leads the meeting each week. Talk about what happened last week. What does everyone need more help with? What's on the calendar for the coming week? Are there any financial considerations on the horizon? It's not business-y; it's about family management.

FAMILY COUNCIL SAMPLE AGENDA[IP]

Adapt the following for Sunday evening or whenever your crew is already together:

1. Gather & Open: Welcome, begin with a family prayer.
2. Quick Gratitude Round: Everyone shares one win or highlight from the past week.
3. Mini-Lesson or Story: Rotate who brings a five-minute lesson or story to share.
4. Calendar Check: Review upcoming commitments: sports, music lessons, piano, youth group activities, work travel, big exams, or school projects.
5. Trip and Vacation Planning: Talk through upcoming getaways, dates, packing lists, activities each person hopes to do, and how to prepare.
6. Family Goals Progress: Check on shared and individual goals and progress, ask for and offer to help each other.
7. Finances and Stewardship: Age-appropriate discussion of money, expenses, work or business updates.
8. Service and Ministry: Discuss opportunities for service to neighbors or friends in need.
9. Home Projects and Chores: List chores and make sure kids are completing their daily work.

10. Spotlights: One family member per week gets extra time to share goals, worries, or something they are excited about.

11. Tech and Screen-Time Review: Briefly review how the family tech plan is working and set any needed limits or challenges for the week.

12. Fun and Adventure: Plan one memory-making activity— game night, beach morning, hike, movie.

13. Commitments Recap: Someone restates who is doing what by when.

14. Closing Prayer & Treat: End with gratitude and a simple dessert treat or short game, so family council stays something everyone looks forward to.

Hold this gathering consistently, keep it brief, and rotate leadership, so every voice matters. Over time, this becomes an opportunity to connect and communicate in an elevated way. And eventually, gathering and discussing ways to help each other just becomes natural.

CHALLENGE: THE TWENTY-FOUR-HOUR EXCUSES DETOX[IP]

Purpose: Excuses impede progress, and they're everywhere. What could you accomplish if you removed them from your life? Good news: you can. You just have to commit and actually do it.

Step 1: Commit to taking a twenty-four-hour excuses detox. No ifs, ands, or buts.

Step 2: If you get stuck, ask yourself: Who do you know who is really good at not making excuses? Connect with that person, and see what you can learn from them.

Step 3: Embrace the discomfort. This might be uncomfortable, but it's supposed to be.

Why it Works: When you go beyond embracing discomfort and actually invest in it, that's where the real magic lies. Combine that with zero excuses, and you've got a recipe for exponential growth.

KEY TAKEAWAYS

▸ Doing well at work and having a family aren't mutually exclusive.

▸ When you're not focused on your own problems and you're Fully Invested in helping other people solve their problems, you're a lot happier.

▸ There's plenty of sacrifice in a Fully Invested life, but if you stay driven by the mission, you won't sacrifice what matters most. You'll sacrifice the stuff that matters least—your time wasters and addictions. You'll also maximize your ability to delegate, so that work keeps happening even when you're not the one doing it.

▸ When in doubt, ask yourself, "What would a Fully Invested leader do in my situation?"

CHAPTER 4

Get Great at Saying No

Most decisions are not a battle between good and bad. Those are easy calls. The tougher choices pit good against better, and better against best. Dallin H. Oaks, an American religious leader and academic, taught the good-better-best filter, and it has become my favorite decision-making tool. Once you know what is best, you can gladly sacrifice what is merely good.

> *Once you know what is best,*
> *you can gladly sacrifice what is*
> *merely good.*

Let me give you an example: Recently, I was hired to speak at a founder's conference for entrepreneurs in Miami, Florida. I was the first keynote speaker, so I spoke from 8:30 to 9:45 a.m. The organizers invited me to stay the whole day and night, including a yacht excursion out on the ocean. They offered to pay for my hotel room for a couple of nights and said they'd love to have me join them for the weekend.

Chad speaking on stage in Florida, 2025

At the conclusion of my talk, there was a break in the conference. A bunch of people in the crowd came up to me to connect and share their insights from my speech. It was fulfilling, and some potentially great new business contacts were made. Then the break ended, and I sat down to listen to the next speaker. As I sat through the next presentation, I thought about what was going on at home that weekend versus the conference yacht party and festivities. And I realized, *You know what? If I leave right now, I'll make it home in time to watch my son's volleyball tournament in Huntington Beach, California.*

He's a senior in high school, and if I attended that tournament, I wouldn't have missed any of his games the entire tournament. Would leaving the conference then mean missing the big boat reception and all the attention that would bring me? Yes. I might miss out on new business opportunities. Plus, what would the organizers think of me for bailing and telling them to cancel the hotel reservation?

In the end, I decided I didn't care as much about what they thought as I did about what my son Pierce thought. I thanked them for inviting (and paying) me to speak and told them I was heading back to California. I didn't even stay for the conference lunch. I left at eleven and made it home to California before three p.m., drove directly from the airport to my son's game, and grabbed a seat in the bleachers two minutes before the match started. The excited look on his face proved far more valuable than any business opportunity that might have come from staying at the conference.

Staying as planned would have been a *good* choice, right? If I got new clients, it would have been an even *better* one. But I decided the *best* thing was to be there for my son's volleyball match to show him that no matter what, I'm always supporting him.

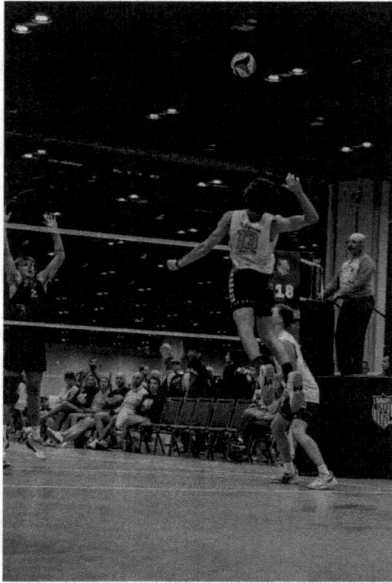

*Pierce flying high at Nationals in
Orlando, Florida, 2025*

*Chad, Pierce, and Amber after Pierce
broke all-time high school records in 2025*

NO SPACE FOR EXCUSES

As a Fully Invested leader, you can't let excuses breathe, not at work and not at home. Reframe what's possible, and you'll dodge the traps that hurt your key relationships. If the calendar says there is no slot for your child's game, you make a slot. Decide how to spend your time based on what matters most, not on how other people might judge your choice.

> *Decide how to spend your time based on what matters most, not on how other people might judge your choice.*

Learning to say no is part of that discipline. Living Fully Invested does not mean you say yes to every request. Early in my career, I tried the yes-to-everything strategy because I was afraid of missing an opportunity or offending a host. I ran to every business mixer and breakfast meeting. It looked ambitious on paper, but I overcommitted and had spread myself too thin.

Overcommitment can feel noble. Many people confuse a packed schedule with true progress. When I hear an entrepreneur brag about how slammed they are, I know they are living in reactive mode, and their lack of schedule discipline does not impress me.

Denzel Washington said it perfectly: "Don't confuse movement with progress." Activity alone is not the goal. Choose with intention, protect what matters, and let every no give more weight to your best yes.

NOT BALANCE, ALIGNMENT

I started my career at Merrill Lynch, and that experience was my first clue that work-life balance was a lie. The number of required meetings and amount of wasted time at this big Wall Street bank nauseated me because I was acutely aware of all the other more impactful things I could be doing. Because I was an employee, I had to engage in the unproductive system they created. That tension of bureaucracy and waste was one of the catalysts for me leaving to start my own business. Instead of playing someone else's game, I saw that I could play my own game and win for our clients with less red tape.

What's the alternative to "balance?" The answer is alignment. It's both more achievable and more satisfying.

Alignment starts internally and flows from your purpose as the driving force, whereas balance lets the external world dictate your life. If you allow external forces to dictate what you spend time, energy, and attention on, you'll find yourself drowning in distractions and constantly reacting to new demands. All those fires you put out might feel urgent, but they're unlikely to be as important as your purpose.

What you think is impossible is *not* impossible. If you believe you don't have time, it's because you're not in alignment. You're trying to live your life from the outside in, not the inside out. You're letting the world tell you what you should be doing.

Your life isn't a pie chart. If you're looking at it that way, trying to divide up the pie into slices of work, home, and other concerns, you'll always fall short. The outer world will decide the size of your pieces, and there will never be enough.

When you instead proceed from alignment, you're working from the inside out. Unexpected challenges will continue to arise, but you'll have a strong foundation of core principles to guide you.

If you're striving to be in "balance," you'll end up trying to juggle too many things and let other people dictate everything about your life. That externally directed existence is a form of learned helplessness.

Recently, I went on a long walk with a Pacific Capital client who founded a business that's now worth billions of dollars. He asked me to join him on this walk because he wanted personal advice beyond our meeting (which included three other team members of mine). His primary questions were around the areas of his life that he felt were slipping. He shared that his personal health was not in a good spot, and he felt he was not able to give his family as much time as he'd like to. His primary concern was that going for his next big business goal was only going to further put his life "out of balance."

We talked about work-life integration, delegation, alignment, and how he could instead reshift his daily schedule to be more Fully

Invested in family and personal health. I told him I was going to send this manuscript over to him as soon as it's finished because this is exactly what he's searching for! Work-life balance is not a real thing. Work-life alignment and integration are absolutely a thing. When you're aligned and integrated, you've got more clarity and strength, knowing what matters more is where you're headed, rather than how fast you're getting there. You're able to focus on the bigger picture instead of the small fires to put out.

> *Work-life balance is not a real thing. Work-life alignment and integration are absolutely a thing.*

WHEN TO SAY NO

You might be wondering: *Okay, I get it, but how do I decide what to say no to?*

Great question.

Go back to that filter of good, better, best. Use your core values to determine whether the opportunity aligns with your top priorities and what you really want. When I had the chance to stay at the conference or leave to attend my son's game, for example, I could have let the external world and the expectations of others dictate my actions—leading to a combination of guilt, confusion, and resentment. When I started from the value of being 100 percent there for my kids in their important moments, though, the choice was obvious and simple.

I weighed my options and made a strategic choice. There was no reason to worry about the "what ifs" around losing hypothetical business opportunities. My business is strong and growing, and the top priority that weekend was my son's tournament. I felt better about what I was saying yes to than what I was saying no to. I love this quote from Josh Billings: "Half of the troubles of this life can be traced to saying yes too quickly and not saying no soon enough."[4] Couldn't agree more.

Making decisions around work tends to be easier. You can choose the most lucrative or impactful opportunity when you have multiple potential deals. Choosing among competing priorities at home may seem harder, but the basic principles are the same. You can choose to show up for your child instead of working through the night.

In a family setting, look at the long-term impact of a difficult choice, and talk to your spouse. If multiple kids have important needs at the same time, talk through the options and make the best choice you can. Maybe you and your spouse each go to an event separately instead of attending together. It's easier to make the choices if you've already built a strong foundation of trust with your kids, so they know they can rely on you.

CALENDAR = COMMITMENT

Most people use their calendar as a "must" for work but don't use it for home—or allow themselves to get double-booked with home events. Your calendar should reflect your most important priorities. You'd never just be a no-show for a business meeting with clients or colleagues, so why would you ever do that for a family occasion? If you're all in at home, then blocking out your home commitments on your integrated calendar is also a must.

The number one reason so many entrepreneurs have broken families and failing marriages is because they are only calendaring and prioritizing business activities.

They're workaholics. If you're like most entrepreneurs, then 90 percent of the commitments on your calendar are work-related. That's a problem. It's a problem because you're scheduling no time for your family, yourself, and your spouse or significant other. I see this all the time, and it leads to burnout and relationship conflict.

There's a tendency to say, "I've got to grind. I have to build. Everyone and everything else can wait." Yet at the same time, you're letting everything at home crumble. Your health is getting worse, your energy is down, and you've got deep resentment and guilt on the inside. I don't think that's what you actually want. And because it's not what you want, you need to do things differently. You have to actually prioritize what matters at home. You need to set aside time for your spouse, for your personal health, for your children. Put those commitments on the calendar.

As an entrepreneur myself, I understand that if I don't schedule something, it won't happen. Too much is coming at me all the time—calls, texts, emails, meetings, Zooms, business opportunities, new investment ideas, and speaker requests. You'll always have demands coming at you for work. If you don't first block out time for your family and follow through, those times to connect with family won't happen. And that creates a problem.

I used to utilize Outlook for my main calendar because it was connected to my work email, and my executive assistant and team members could view it, putting commitments on there when there were openings. But in 2018, I switched to Google Calendar, where I'd add family and personal commitments first. Then, when business opportunities came up, my team would consult with my executive assistant to see if a personal or family commitment was scheduled, and they could add a business appointment. We basically flipped the process upside down. I would no longer bail on personal or family commitments for business. Instead, I would ask for different times or days to meet, so I could be Fully Invested at home. This integrated calendar has changed my life.

6 AM	Weightlifting Session w/ Trainer 5:45 – 6:45am
7 AM	Family Devotional and Breakfast, 7am
	Drop Off Sterling and Carpool School, 7:30am
8 AM	
9 AM	Goal Planning Zoom Appt w/ EAs 8:30 – 9:30am
10 AM	Podcast Recording in Studio 10 – 11am
11 AM	Client Call w/ The Smiths, 11am
12 PM	Client Lunch Meeting (Newport Beach) 12 – 1pm
1 PM	
2 PM	Edit Forbes Articles, 1:30pm
	Book Editing Call w/ Publisher, 2pm
3 PM	Leadership Training w/ Executive Team 3 – 4pm
4 PM	
5 PM	Bentley's Volleyball Practice 4:30 – 5:30pm
6 PM	Family Dinner Time 6 – 7pm
7 PM	
8 PM	Sterling Basketball Practice 7:15 – 8:15pm

What most ambitious business leaders get wrong is that family life and business are not a trade-off situation. The conventional wisdom would be either/or, but a Fully Invested life is both/and. By reorganizing your approach to how you calendar, you can find the ways to win big in your business and at home.

For example, our family treats Sunday as a unique day of the week. Sundays, for us, are days of worship, rest, service, and family time. We keep it simple with four Rs: reflect, reset, reunite, and rest. Those are our priorities that center our first day of the week. Now that we have such a busy life with five kids, we say no to work, personal entertainment, exercise, meetings, and other commitments on Sunday. By saying no, we gain more power. By carving out space and time away from our normal daily activities, we recharge ourselves for the week ahead, both for work and home life.

Pierce, Bentley, McKinley, Chad, Beckham, Amber, and Sterling at Sunday church, 2024

Whether you take Sundays for rest or not, the point is the same: your calendar reflects your priorities. What's on yours?

> *I absolutely calendar my family commitments to set them in stone as I would any important business meeting. My family knows that they are my top priority and the main driver behind any success I am able to achieve outside of our home. I want my wife and children to know that they are my ultimate "why" for everything I do and have learned that I can only achieve peak performance in my work life if all is well with my family.*
>
> **–JUSTIN DALTON,**
> **ENTREPRENEUR AND WASTE MANAGEMENT INDUSTRY INVESTOR**

CHOOSING WISELY

About a decade ago, someone referred a potential client to me who, at $120 million, would have been my largest ever client by 400 percent. As you can imagine, I was very excited. He originally contacted *me*; I didn't pursue him, which made the whole possibility feel even more special. My team and I met with him multiple times via online calls. As we got to know him, he seemed very sharp, but also somewhat demanding and demeaning toward the team, particularly the women who work with me.

As the meetings continued, I noticed that he seemed rude and high-maintenance, and I pictured him being difficult to deal with as a long-term client. On the surface, the amount of revenue we stood to gain seemed worth dealing with his strong personality and demanding style. We could put up with some tough expectations; we could make it work. But deep down, I knew I wouldn't be the one managing his account day to day; if I agreed to take him on, my team would have to deal with him, and I'd be giving that burden mostly to them.

I thought about it over the weekend and realized, despite the financial incentives, there was no way we should take him on as a new client because he'd cause a lot of stress and trouble.

In the end, I politely let him know he'd probably find a better fit elsewhere, and we weren't the right team for him. How'd he react? He was shocked! Nobody tells this guy they don't want to work with him. He got upset and insulted, and that was the last time we spoke. But how did my team feel about this hard decision? They were so relieved, and their morale and energy were boosted. They'd been anticipating dealing with this person, but then they saw I stood for principles and said no to protect their well-being. I could've gotten away with making him my team's problem, sure, but that wouldn't have felt right. After I made the decision to pass, they had my back even more. This proves that saying no can be just as important, if not more, than saying yes.

ALWAYS CONSIDER THE PAYOFF

Every yes is a tradeoff in one way or another. That goes back to the idea of choice and empowerment, rather than being powerless in the face of external demands. As Tim Ferriss says, "What you *don't* do determines what you *can* do."[5]

The payoff of saying no and prioritizing your family is preserving your best energy and best effort for the people and activities that matter most, rather than giving your work or your family your leftovers.

Instead of always trying to juggle more commitments, it's more fulfilling to live in alignment, choose what fits with your highest priorities, and say no to the rest. When people talk about how they "have to" or "should" do something, it sounds powerless and helpless, like you're somehow tied to the outside world's expectations. Instead, focus on what you are *choosing* to do, given all the possible ways to spend your time. Steve Jobs famously taught, "Focus is about saying no."

A clear and confident no earns you more respect than a reluctant yes. We have clear parameters around the kinds of clients we do and don't work with. For instance, we don't work with professional athletes. I was referred to a top NBA basketball player recently. It was difficult to say no because I'm a diehard NBA fan. Basketball is a big part of our family, and all the opportunities flashed in my imagination about working with a bunch of NBA guys. However, I know deep down inside that our Pacific Capital family office team is uniquely designed for high-level entrepreneurs, not professional athletes. And by continually saying no to great opportunities outside our specialty zone, we become more powerful for the right-fit clients. And just like the $120 million client we rejected, this NBA referral source had a very surprised reaction when we declined the opportunity. But it wasn't even a hard decision. When you're clear about what you want, you get better at saying no to what falls outside your mission.

> *A clear and confident no earns*
> *you more respect than*
> *a reluctant yes.*

FULLY INVESTED FRAMEWORKS: SAYING NO

BEFORE WE MEET

Being Fully Invested means you cannot say yes to everything, as we've learned, and that includes every meeting request. I created a meeting request form that our ELEVATED community members use to make sure priorities and energy are optimized. Take a look and try it out yourself!

Fully Invested

ELEVATED
FULLY INVESTED™

PLEASE NOTE:

My time and attention are focused on my most important priorities: my family, clients, and current team members. Because of this, I'm often unable to accept meeting requests. To help us evaluate potential value and alignment of your meeting request, please complete this "Before We Meet" worksheet.

CLIENT INFORMATION:

Full Name: _____ **E-Mail:** _____

Phone #: _____ **Company / Position / Title:** _____

WHAT'S THE PRIMARY PURPOSE OF THIS MTG & WHAT DO YOU HOPE TO ACHIEVE?

WHAT BENEFITS & VALUE DO YOU EXPECT US EACH TO GAIN FROM THIS MEETING?

Could this meeting be accomplished with a well written email? ☐ No ☐ Yes

Are you a client of mine? ☐ No ☐ Yes

Is preparation required before the meeting on my end? ☐ No ☐ Yes, please explain

PLEASE SHARE ANY ADDITIONAL CONTEXT YOU THINK WOULD BE HELPFUL.

WE APPRECIATE YOUR TIME & WILL BE IN TOUCH SHORTLY.

For a downloadable copy of the Before We Meet worksheet and other resources, scan the QR code below:

WAKE UP AND WIN

Set intentions before you go to bed. If you know what you want to say yes to tomorrow, it will be easier to say no to the things that pop up that aren't aligned with your priorities. "If you don't plan your day, someone or something else will," Nir Eyal said.[6]

Priorities can evolve over time. Your main focus may not be the same in Q1 as in Q3. Similarly, priorities can also change within families. If one of your kids is about to graduate from high school, then a priority will likely be helping them get into college. If one of your kids is struggling with mental health, then you'll prioritize getting them the support they need sooner, not later.

There are different seasons when you need to invest more in one area of your life than another, or in one child than another. Everything has its time and season. If you just started your business, you may need to focus on client acquisition before booking a few big family vacations.

Regardless of the cycle of your business, though, you can prioritize being present. And that starts with setting intentions. Before you go to bed, write down three intentions for the next day.

Small task, big results.

Don't take my word for it, the famous success guru Jim Rohn said, "Never begin the day until it is finished on paper."[7]

Wake Up & Win™   ELE√ATED

Tomorrow's Date & Wake Up Time:

EXCITEMENT & ENERGY	What's exciting about tomorrow?
TOP FOCUS OF YOUR DAY	What are you focused on and what does winning look like?

PERSONAL WIN

WHAT'S THE BEST PERSONAL WIN YOU'LL ACHIEVE?

BUSINESS WIN

WHAT'S THE BEST BUSINESS WIN YOU'LL ACHIEVE?

WIN

WAKE UP & WIN MOMENTUM CREATORS: FIRST 3 THINGS I WILL DO

01

02

03

DESCRIBE HOW YOUR WAKE UP & WIN STRATEGY WORKED THIS MORNING. KEEP YOURSELF ACCOUNTABLE.

DON'T SKIP THIS SECTION.

CHALLENGE: THE CALENDAR FACELIFT[IP]

Purpose: Too often, we only have work commitments on our calendars. If you're a Fully Invested leader, that stops now. Next week, calendar time for your family and your health. Block it off and take the commitment as seriously as you would a client meeting.

> **Step 1**: Next week, calendar time for your family. If your child has a game or event, block it on your calendar. Add a date night with your spouse.

> **Step 2:** Next week, calendar time for your health and well-being. If you decide to commit to doing a workout program, for example, put it on your calendar.

Why It Works: What you focus on grows. If you open your calendar every day and see these family and health commitments, you're reinforcing their importance. Hold true to yourself rather than letting the outside world push you around.

KEY TAKEAWAYS

▸ We often think choices are between good and bad, but that's not usually the case. Those choices are easy. The harder ones are between good, better, and best.

▸ What's the alternative to "balance?" The answer is alignment. It's both more achievable and more satisfying.

▸ The number one reason so many entrepreneurs have broken families and failing marriages is because they are only calendaring business activities.

▸ Saying no can be just as important, if not more, than saying yes.

The payoff of saying no and prioritizing your family is preserving your best energy and best effort for the people and activities that matter most, rather than giving your work or your family your leftovers.

CHAPTER 5

Activate Strengths, Amplify Alignment

We don't give our kids a cell phone until they're sixteen years old, which (as you might have guessed) makes me the meanest dad in town. Back when our oldest daughter (now almost twenty-one) was in seventh grade, she was literally the only child at her middle school without a phone. One kid out of twelve hundred. She was, to put it mildly, not happy about it.

"You're thirteen," I told her back then. "You've got three more years to wait. You don't need a phone at this age anyway. I didn't even have a phone as a married college student!" We did not agree on this at all.

But four months into the school year, I was driving her to basketball practice and she said something that really surprised me:

"I'm actually glad I don't have a cell phone."

"Whoa, seriously?" I said. "Why?"

"Because at lunch, everyone sits there like a robot with their AirPods looking down at the screen, doing nothing and saying nothing. It's so boring. Nobody cares about anyone around them, just what's on their phone screen. There's nobody to talk to. So I go shoot hoops on the playground."

Looking back at that situation now, eight years later, I realize what an impact that had on McKinley! It's evident that she developed a lot of strengths by avoiding the smartphone addiction that many of her young peers and friends fell into. She became a better communicator, able to start and carry conversations with adults, teachers, coaches, and friends at a higher level than her peers. She got into creative arts, becoming a great painter and poet. McKinley even wrote a poem that was published and won her a county award. She took piano and after-school Spanish lessons, eventually earned the National Seal of Bi-literacy in high school, and started a basketball training clinic out of our backyard that earned her $170 per hour at its peak, eventually leading to her playing basketball at a division one college. And the list goes on. Would she have accomplished and experienced all of this if we handed her a smartphone at thirteen like her friends' parents? Absolutely not.

I'm not here to pretend my wife and I are perfect parents, to rail against cell phones, or tell you when your child should or should not get one. That's your personal decision, and one I encourage you to make it thoughtfully. But I *am* here to say that McKinley is an example of discovering strengths and *leveraging* them. For a minute, think about the value of your attention. A thirty-second commercial during the latest Super Bowl cost upwards of $5 million! Why would a company pay $5 million for a thirty-second ad on TV? Because we live in the attention economy. If that's how much the world values your attention, then you should value it *even more*.

In our house and in my businesses, we choose to put our attention on our strengths.

This isn't always as easy breezy as it sounds. But there are times when this focus produces almost magical results. For example, when my team member Esty applied to be a coach at ELEVATED, she contacted us through the general support email address, and her message got overlooked. By the time we found her résumé a month later, we'd already hired someone for that specific coaching role. I didn't have a spot open for her right then, but her client engagement experience was so impressive that I figured it was at least worth a conversation.

During our FaceTime interview call, she talked about how she'd recently worked for a coaching company that the leader abruptly shut down, even though it was doing well. That left her out of a job and extremely disappointed. She loved her career and the industry, but she decided to follow her childhood dream of becoming a dentist like her dad, with the hopes of taking over his dental practice someday.

She enrolled in Utah State University to finish the last few prerequisites required to apply to dental school and was on her first day when we had our call. I asked, "What lights you up? What are you really excited about? What do you want to do in the future?" She felt like she *should* be a dentist, but I didn't hear any fire or excitement in her voice. Her true passions were growth, goal-setting, marketing, connecting with new people, and self-improvement.

"Okay," I said, "how many hours a week could you dedicate if I found a spot for you on our member engagement team?" She showed me her packed school schedule, which was going to stretch for several more years before she could eventually become a dentist. "How are you going to work for me if your entire schedule is full of classes?" I asked. "That's not going to work. Are you 100 percent sure you want to be a dentist?"

"I want to have a great and fulfilling career," she said. "I want to grow. I want to learn new things, to be rewarded for my efforts and contribution, and I also want to be a mom and have kids."

"Respectfully," I told her, "the goals you're describing are not super achievable as a dentist." She could earn lots of money someday (after a decade of additional schooling and apprenticeship), but she'd spend long hours in the clinic doing dental work to earn that pay. Where would the kids fit in? Based on her assessments and interview answers, I could tell she wouldn't be fully satisfied with that path. Deep down, it wasn't really where she wanted to be.

I laid out what her life could look like if she decided to work for our member service team at ELEVATED. She could mold the position based on her strengths and passions and be rewarded based on how she helped entrepreneurial leaders grow.

She said she'd talk to her husband, and guess what? An hour later, she got back to me. Even though she'd gone through the whole process of enrolling in dental school and was already in the middle of her first week of classes, she dropped out then and there. She abandoned that ill-fitting path and became the epitome of Fully Invested in our ELEVATED community. And you should hear the feedback we get from members about how much of a positive impact she makes on them!

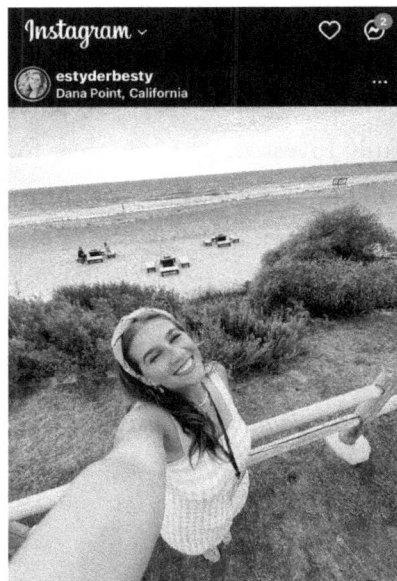

Esty Angel, ELEVATED team member

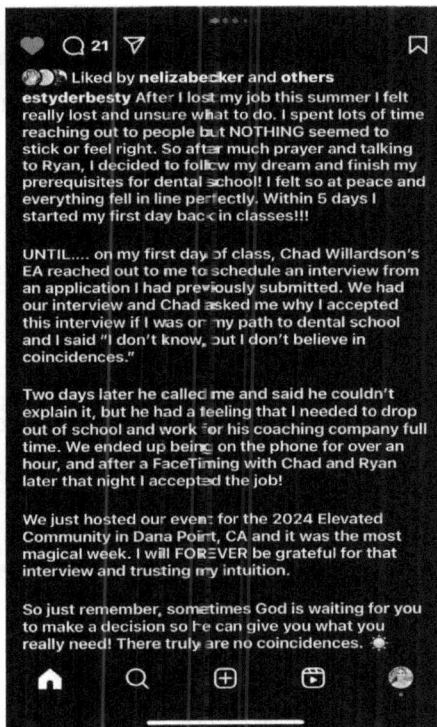

Though it was a big pivot, the timing worked out perfectly. If we'd spoken two months earlier, when she originally emailed, she might have always had the lingering question about whether she actually should have become a dentist. Instead, she got to commit to that dental path and was open to then be redirected to a better career fit for her goals. She had to make that decision and begin down the road to learn and feel that it was the wrong fit, whereas the coaching community opportunity lit her up. Here's a great reminder: Google Maps, Waze, and GPS don't guide parked cars. You've got to be moving forward before you can get clarity on what shifts and adjustments to make on the way to your destination. So get moving!

All the ELEVATED members love Esty, and she's already grown so much. She takes initiative and has created many new ways to engage new members and support existing members because we've given her the space to do so. As a result, she's Fully Invested, which is great for her and great for everyone else, too—all because of our strengths-first approach.

> *If you watch your team succeed and fail, that can help identify strengths. The best practice is to watch what they gravitate toward when put under pressure. That will be their strongest attribute.*
>
> **—CASEY ADAMS,
> ENTREPRENEUR AND FOUNDER**

THE RIGHT INSTINCT FOR THE ROLE

The best way to ride a horse is in the direction it is already running. I try to do the same with people. When someone joins my team, I look for the type of work that already lights them up and then shape the role to expand that strength. No one should wake up on Monday and dread the work week ahead.

In my businesses, we hire slowly. A mix of interviews and instinct assessments helps us discover how a candidate thinks, what fuels them, and what drains them. Once they are in the door, my job is to coach and give them room to grow inside their genius zone.

Those instinct profiles and interview questions vary by role. A portfolio analyst needs different wiring than a client-facing tax strategist or a membership engagement specialist. I've learned this the hard way. Any time I ignored the assessment results and trusted a good interview alone, I later regretted it.

A new job candidate asked me today if she had "passed" the four tests we use. But there is no pass or fail. The results simply tell us where her energy spikes and where it slumps.

Some startups say, "If you're a culture fit, we will find you a seat." I take the opposite view. I know the seats I need. Then I hire people whose instincts and skillsets match those seats. Culture matters, but it doesn't override the need for the right person in the right chair.

FOSTERING ALIGNMENT AT HOME

In the family setting, leveraging natural strengths and supporting each other comes from getting to know your family members as individuals. No two kids are alike, and even siblings growing up in the same household will have very distinct strengths and interests. For instance, our oldest daughter, McKinley, is a great connector and very social. She loves to be right where the action is; big events feed her energy. She loves public speaking and talking with people she's never met. She loves being spontaneous and finds new adventures and challenges exciting. Those activities light her up. By contrast, she's not mechanical and doesn't enjoy fixing things. She and I are quite alike in those ways.

Our oldest son, Pierce, is also an excellent public speaker, yet he comes at it from a more analytical perspective. He's headed to college to study business and astrophysics and would someday want to work with NASA. He has a completely different brain; he is a deep thinker who doesn't feel the need to be at every big event where the action is, like his older sister McKinley. He's a strategist. Pierce's favorite school subjects were astronomy, physics, and math. I remember when Pierce was just two or three years old and already taking apart his new remote-controlled cars that he got for Christmas. He wanted to see how they worked on the inside and then put them back together. Though wearing diapers, he was probably already more mechanical and better with tools than I was in my thirties!

Our middle son and middle child, Sterling, is one of the most social people we've ever met! He has the ability to connect, build, and maintain friendships with people from every background. He remembers names and faces and generally makes people feel comfortable. Sterling is also insanely disciplined. For three years in a middle school boot camp academy, he kept track of every meal, tracked his macros and his workouts, and trained like he was already a college athlete. He's a gentle giant at six foot eight and two hundred thirty pounds, entering the ninth grade, and is endearing to all with his great sense of humor.

Our second daughter, Bentley, has the sweetest personality and is naturally full of emotional intelligence. At age three, she could sense if someone was having a bad day and would want to give them a hug. She's always had a sense for being a peacemaker. Bentley is also incredibly gifted with excellent hand-eye coordination and is gifted on the piano. She can play nearly any piece with grace and skill—plus, she is a talented artist and an outstanding volleyball setter. She's also naturally thoughtful and the first one to say "thank you" or write a thank-you card.

Our youngest child, Beckham, is one in a million. Beckham just turned ten and is one of the wittiest ten-year-olds on planet Earth. A little Einstein. Like Pierce, he's got a mechanical engineer's type of brain. He's a real thinker. Beckham has a blend of traits from my wife and me and all four of his older siblings. When he was assessed for kindergarten, the school counselor told us he was already reading at a fifth-grade level. We all like to joke that Beckham is the smartest one in the family, even at his young age. But he's also emotionally intelligent and is picking up on everything—said and unsaid. I can't wait to see what Beckham turns out to do with his talents!

As you can see, each of our five kids has some traits in common beyond their last name, yet they're also unique, much like your kids, I'm sure. Therefore, the support, discipline, encouragement, boundaries, and communication styles they need are not the same. If you try to approach your kids and their distinct personalities in the exact same way, your relationships will suffer, and your connection will be weak.

> *Taking a cookie-cutter approach to your relationships simply doesn't work, whether in your business life or family life.*

Pierce, McKinley, Bentley, Sterling, and Beckham, Balboa Fun Zone, 2024

Taking a cookie-cutter approach to your relationships simply doesn't work, whether in your business life or family life. As a Fully Invested leader, you're willing to put in the extra effort to get to know the important people in your life so well that you can adjust how you communicate and show up for each person.

One of the greatest gifts of parenting and partnering is getting a front-row seat to someone else becoming more of who they are. I deeply admire my husband Sunny's groundedness—his ability to remain calm, thoughtful, and present no matter what's swirling around him. He's a natural simplifier, a systems thinker, and a generous listener. Years ago, I might've seen his deliberateness as frustrating or slowing us down. But now, I recognize how much his strengths balance mine. His thinking makes our ideas sharper, our plans more scalable, and our family life more intentional. Instead of being intimidated by our differences, we've learned to lean on each other's strengths, especially in the places where we individually fall short. That shift—asking for help without shame, seeing strengths as complementary—has strengthened our partnership in every way.

We try to model that same belief with our kids. Each of our children is highly different: one is endlessly curious, one is a free spirit full of imagination, and one is a wild child with a bold, independent spirit and big ideas of his own. Our goal isn't to shape them into a mold—but to help each of them become more of who they already are. We talk a lot in our family about "owning your magic," and that starts with seeing and celebrating each person's uniqueness. We try to honor individual thinking over blind compliance, and we listen— truly listen—to our kids' perspectives. We may not always go with what they want, but they always have a voice and a chance to be heard.

**–ANN C. SHEU,
FOUNDER AND CEO, MPOWERED FAMILIES**

DON'T GENERALIZE–SPECIALIZE!

I'd rather help someone amplify their strengths and interests in alignment with a shared goal than have them struggle and try to get better at their weakness (especially when others out there are already great at it). When you have a team of people specializing at a high level, there's no need to waste time and energy placing them in situations where they'll perform at a mediocre level. Helping your team members become experts and specialists in their areas of natural strengths provides many advantages:

- **Skill Mastery**: When people focus on a narrow set of tasks, they can develop deep expertise and become more efficient.
- **Streamlined Workflows**: Clearly defined roles and responsibilities lead to smoother workflow management, preventing bottlenecks.
- **Better Quality Control:** When employees consistently perform the same specialized tasks, it's easier to identify and address issues, sometimes even before they happen.
- **Sense of Accomplishment:** Focusing on specific tasks can give team members a greater sense of accomplishment, leading to higher job satisfaction and motivation.
- **Reduced Training Expenses:** Focused roles minimize the need for extensive training across multiple areas, keeping training costs low.
- **In-depth Knowledge**: Specialized employees, with their deep understanding of specific areas, are better equipped to identify opportunities for innovation and develop new techniques or technologies.
- **Faster Adaptation**: Experts in their fields can more quickly implement new technologies and methodologies, keeping the business competitive and always ready to adapt.

PLAY TO YOUR STRENGTHS

It's tempting to take on every task yourself, to plug each gap and conquer every weakness, one at a time. But all that really does is scatter your energy, leaving you average at a long list of different things. You can spend years chasing skills that never come naturally while ignoring the gifts that do.

The difference between my skills and my in-laws' skills is a good example of this. Her dad was a dentist, two brothers are chiropractors, another brother works with concrete, and her sister is a nurse. They all use their hands for work, and they're great at it. I'd be terrible at any of those jobs. My work lives in my head and in my spoken words. I'm all about ideas, vision, strategy, relationships, communication, and so on. Give me a phone, and I can run my business from anywhere because it's work between the ears and not with my hands. To them, it probably doesn't even look like work because I never break a sweat.

Even after we married, I believe some of my new relatives were a bit puzzled by what I did for a living because no one in their world had ever sat at a desk and talked for a paycheck. Ask me to fix a leak or build a new bookshelf, and you might as well ask me to write poetry in Mandarin.

At first, Amber found it strange (lazy) that I hired people to handle repairs or assembly projects. She felt the "man of the house" should handle those jobs. She also probably didn't realize how challenging and subpar it would turn out if I had tried to do it. Now we agree that my time and energy belong where I can create the most value for our family. I can struggle for twelve hours to build a cabinet or pay a professional $200 to finish it in ninety minutes. The pro enjoys the work, does it better, and I stay fresh for the work only I can do.

I believe everyone has one or two gifts that can be world-class, not twenty-five. The faster we admit what they are and stay in that lane, the better life runs. I focus on mine, you focus on yours, and the results multiply.

My assistants keep a running list of experts we rely on: photographer, plumber, trainer, chef, editor, mechanic, pilots, and more. Each is an all-star in their field. I do not want to be a jack-of-all-trades. I want to be Fully Invested in the work that only I can do and let other specialists shine in theirs.

> *Figuring out what people are truly great at begins with listening. I pay close attention to what energizes them, where they lose track of time, and what others naturally come to them for. Then I design roles around strengths, not job titles. When people operate from their zone of genius, they do not just perform; they flourish.*
>
> **–NINAD TIPNIS,**
> **FOUNDER AND PRINCIPAL, JTCPL DESIGNS**

LEVERAGING EXECUTIVE ASSISTANTS

In service of activating strengths and amplifying success, it's important for a Fully Invested leader to find the right assistant(s). I've been able to free up significant time in business and family life by hiring two excellent full-time assistants. A prominent entrepreneur conference in Florida even invited me to speak at their annual summit about how I've leveraged that two-assistant structure.

Having assistants helps us win big in business and at home. For instance, while I'm writing this book at the kitchen table, I can hear my wife on the phone brainstorming with my personal assistant

Oriya to coordinate the logistics of our upcoming family vacation to Peru.

I know what you're thinking: *Two assistants, though? Really? That sounds crazy. Who even needs that?* Well, let me tell you how they work. One focuses strictly on business and financial matters, and the other on personal matters. Basically, one supports my left brain, and the other supports my right brain.

ELEVATED PACIFIC CAPITAL

**Entrepreneurs:
Stop Scaling Alone**

Join ELEVATED - the Growth-Focused
Network That Helps Leaders Grow Beyond
7 & 8 Figures Without Working More

SCHEDULE YOUR DISCOVERY CALL

LINK IN BIO

Oriya Hirschhorn · 1st
Personal Executive Assistant to Chad Willardson
United States · Contact info
https://chadwillardson.com/

PACIFIC CAPITAL

California State University,
Northridge

As a Fully Invested leader, you should consider a similar setup. After our presentation at that conference in Florida a few years ago, I've seen many friends and business associates follow this pattern. Once your business has reached a level of success, you can afford creating a success support team for your businesses and your family. It's now a matter of trust, collaboration, and creating more freedom from things that slow you down.

Kylee Stevens ✓ · 1st   PACIFIC CAPITAL
Business Executive Assistant to Chad Willardson
United States · Contact info
https://chadwillardson.com/

Schedule Your Call with Us

There's been a huge shift in how I handle delegating compared to the previous five years to the twenty-five-year period before that. For the first twenty-five years, I focused on delegating one major thing per quarter. As a result of that period of time, I 25X'd my income. The shift in the last five years is that I am now so clear on how I should be spending my time. I don't take on anything that doesn't fit, so I don't have to go through the heavy lifting of beginning those tasks and responsibilities and someday delegating them. I simply start the process by making sure there's someone to do that work so I stay in my sweet spot right out of the chute. This applies to everything, be it taking on a new project, starting a new company, or pursuing any new endeavor. In the past, it was about chipping things away; now it is all about staying in my sweet spot.

–GINO WICKMAN,
AUTHOR OF TRACTION & SHINE, CREATOR OF EOS®

FULLY INVESTED FRAMEWORK: ACTIVATE STRENGTHS

THE EXECUTIVE ASSISTANT HIRING GUIDE

Your EA can transform your life. Here's how to find and collaborate with the right one (or ones, if you have multiple):

- Delegate effectively. (Use clear instructions and expectations.)
- Set Clear KPIs. (Define what success looks like for each EA.)
- Use the right tools (Slack, Asana, Trello, and shared calendars).
- Encourage professional growth (courses, mentorship, and feedback loops).
- Foster teamwork. (Keep your EAs aligned through shared goals.)

Pro tip: If your EA doesn't know your top three priorities at all times, your delegation process is broken!

The form below will give you an idea of what you can expect from the right-fit EA:

WHAT DOES AN EA DO?

WHAT AN EA SHOULD NOT BE ❌	WHAT AN EA SHOULD BE ✅
A task-taker with no context: Executes without understanding your goals—zero strategic value.	**A Strategic Extension of You:** Anticipates your needs, aligns with your thinking.
An Administrative Crutch: Relieves pressure short-term, but creates long-term drag.	**An Architect of Leverage:** Builds systems that multiply your time and output.
A Passive Operator: Waits for instructions instead of thinking ahead.	**A Focus Protector:** Shields you from noise and low-value distractions.
A Micromanagement Drain: Needs constant oversight— costs you time and trust.	**A Trusted Proxy:** Represents you in meetings and messaging with confidence.
	A Decision Accelerator: Preps options and context so you act fast and smart.
	A Hub for Ops and Relationships: Keeps people, projects, and processes running smoothly.
	An Accountability Mirror: Holds you to your priorities— personally and professionally.

chad
willardson

An EA is not just an assistant—they're a **game changer**!

ELEVATE AND THRIVE

Use this template to help set clear expectations for anyone who works for you:

ELEVATE AND THRIVE™ ELEVATED FULLY INVESTED™

THIS WORKSHEET PROVIDES CLARITY AND EXTABLISHES EXPECTATIONS FOR YOUR CLIENTS

Name & Position:

COMPETENCIES & SKILLS REQUIRED TO THRIVE IN YOUR ROLE

YOUR PERSONAL STRENGTHS THAT ELEVATE YOUR WORK

SUCCESSFUL RESULTS TO ACHIEVE

ISSUES TO FIX & CAUSES OF FRUSTATION

ADDITIONAL INSIGHTS & EXPECTATIONS

WHERE CLARITY BEGINS, GROWTH FOLLOWS.

CHALLENGE: THE CHEMISTRY CHECK[IP]

Purpose: Find and fix weak points in your team chemistry before they become bigger problems.

Have every team member (or family member) rate the team on these four questions (scaled from 1–10):

- How clear am I on my role and what's expected of me?
- Do I feel valued for my strengths and effort?
- Do I trust the other team members?
- Are my goals aligned with the goals of our team?

Why It Works: This is a great way to gather information about how your team members and family members feel about themselves and their contributions individually and as part of the whole. If someone responds with a low number, take that opportunity to check in. (For tips on how to do that well, see the next chapter on the power of presence.)

KEY TAKEAWAYS

- The best direction to ride a horse is the way the horse is already running. I get to know what people on my business team are great at, what gives them energy, and what excites them, and then I try to focus on those areas and help them expand their responsibilities in those natural strengths.

- In the family setting, leveraging natural strengths comes from getting to know your family members as individuals. No two kids are alike, and even siblings growing up in the same household will have distinct strengths and interests.

- Everyone has one or two things they're amazing at. We should all be honest about what those skills are and specialize in them. As long as we collaborate with each other, everything will still get done, but in a much more enjoyable way.

- It can be tempting to work outside your natural strengths and try to master everything that needs to get done in your life and business, but you'll just end up scattering your energy without achieving results. We could waste our entire lives working on our weaknesses and get nowhere.

- Leverage assistants to help manage your work and home—and yes, those can be separate assistants.

CHAPTER 6

Lead with the Power of Presence

A Fully Invested leader values their attention and therefore gives attention to what they value.

Let me give you an example: we were on Grand Cayman on a family vacation and rented a beach cabana right in front of the ocean. It was a beautiful sunny day, probably 85 degrees, with tropical water and white sand. My family and I played cornhole and beach volleyball and went swimming in the ocean together. My wife and our younger kids even spent some time building sand castles.

By contrast, the guy in the cabana next to us spent every day from 10 a.m. to 5 p.m. working on his laptop. It just looked sad. Why spend all that money to be at a beautiful luxury hotel on an epic island in the Caribbean and use all of your time staring at your phone and laptop? Maybe he had an emergency at work, but for the entire week? The amount of self-importance and false urgency often drives us to be fully present for work and fully absent from our family. You don't have to be connected every moment of every day, especially on your family beach vacation.

Beckham, Amber, Pierce, Sterling, Chad, and Bentley,
Sting Ray City, Cayman Islands, 2025

Most people would think the world was ending if they lost their phone or laptop for a day or two, yet once they found it on the third day, they'd realize it wasn't as big a deal as they had imagined. Too often, we feel a false sense of importance that we need to know everything happening in real time.

When I see someone who's a distracted mess, doesn't manage their attention well, and can't be present in the moment, I always think the rest of their life must be out of whack. *P.S. It's not fun to hang around people like that because they are never actually there with you.*

Presence is like a lighthouse. Imagine if the lighthouse moved every time a ship needed guidance; it would be useless. Ship captains wouldn't know where to look, and sailors would be lost. A lighthouse is a powerful symbol of presence and stability. It doesn't chase after the ships. It doesn't flicker or fade unpredictably. It stands consistently tall and unwavering to guide ships safely through storms, darkness, and uncertainty. Presence is like that, too, both in business and in your family; it requires substance, yielding, service, love, and gratitude.

Presence is more valuable than time. You can spend hours with someone who pays no attention to you and get nothing from it, or you can build a strong connection in a short amount of time with someone who gives you their full attention. How do you feel when the person you're with gives you their full presence?

At the end of the day, your team doesn't need more emails and scattered Slack messages; they need clarity. Your family doesn't need more gifts; they need your attention and presence.

MULTITASKING IS A LIE

How you treat your attention and how present you are will affect everything else in your life, especially your relationships. Multitasking during time to connect is the behavior of someone who's half in, not Fully Invested.

In fact, multitasking is a lie. Your brain can only do one important thing at a time. It's one thing to listen to music while you vacuum; those aren't cognitively demanding tasks. However, you can't fully watch a movie while doing your math homework (though I've seen my teenagers try).

> *Multitasking is a lie. Your brain can only do one important thing at a time.*

In reality, you're just switching back and forth between tasks, and that comes with a cost. Research shows that frequently shifting from one activity to another can deplete as much as 40 percent of your productive time. Once interrupted, workers take on average twenty-three to thirty minutes to fully resume the original task.

The typical person spends almost half of their workday recovering from distractions. The transition and switching times costs are so expensive that they result in the loss of billions of dollars per year for employers. Continuous partial attention (constant switching) is tied to: higher stress, elevated cortisol levels, reduced cognitive flexibility, diminished concentration, and decision fatigue. It also correlates with increased anxiety and lower job satisfaction, particularly in teams.

Given these facts, it's clear that "multitasking" is trying—unsuccessfully—to do two things at the same time and doing both poorly. You'd finish more quickly and achieve a better outcome if you simply focused on one thing, completed it, and then moved on to the next thing. That's why time blocking to batch activities is so effective.

Multitasking is like turning on every faucet in the house at once—trying to shower while brushing your teeth and flushing the toilet. Technically, you can do it all, but the water pressure drops everywhere. Eventually, nothing flows well.

The same happens with your attention. Split focus means diluted results. I encourage my team to work in clear, focused sprints—one meaningful task at a time, done with full presence. That's where real momentum and quality come from.

–LIOR WEINSTEIN,
FOUNDER, CTOX.COM

ELIMINATE DISTRACTIONS

This has been on my mind for two decades. In fact, in March 2010, I was interviewed by *Entrepreneur* magazine (the article was called "E-Mail is Making You Stupid") to share my unique approach to email inbox management.[8] During that interview, I shared how I went from checking my email inbox dozens of times per hour to just four times per day at specific intervals. That interview was fifteen years ago, and I'm happy to say things have improved since then. Today, I have zero notifications or alerts on my phone and my laptop. Zero. People ask me how I know when to check my messages and texts. I check them when I'm ready and choose to do so. If it's an emergency, someone will call. If they can't get in touch with me, they can reach out to my wife or two assistants. If it's that urgent, someone will figure out how to get ahold of me. I'm definitely reachable, just not interruptable.

The conventional way of navigating this overly connected world is a trap. Most people don't control their attention. They react to everything—endless notifications, low-value conversations, social media, news, gossip, viral videos, rabbit holes, and other people's problems. Fully Invested leaders eliminate distractions, refuse unnecessary meetings and time-wasters, and silence interruptions. You can have an amazing day once you step outside your inbox.

> *Fully Invested leaders eliminate distractions, refuse unnecessary meetings and time-wasters, and silence interruptions.*

I have no interest in gossip, entertainment awards shows, Hollywood, or reality TV. Never seen anything on Netflix (really never). Maybe I've missed out on some amazing shows. Or the latest reality TV drama that everyone's talking about. I don't care. I've found people spend a lot of effort and energy worrying about what other people think about them, but in reality, most people aren't thinking about you. They're thinking about themselves.

Since early 2019, I've delegated my work email inbox. I still respond to important clients personally, but 95 percent of the emails that come through are not important and not from our clients. It's been a wonderful relief, and I wish I'd turned off notifications and delegated those responses to my assistant much earlier in my career. That arrangement saves me tons of time. Here's the auto-reponder message that someone receives when they email me:

Hey there,

I'm committed to being fully present with people (more people, less screens), so I may not respond immediately or personally to your email. If your request is urgent, please call our service team (Cori or Katrina) at 844-777-8777. If you're looking to work with our PACIFIC CAPITAL team, please schedule directly on our site.

P.S. If you like reading or listening to audiobooks, my 5 best-selling books are available on Amazon!

Wishing you an amazing day outside the inbox!

Fully Invested,

Chad

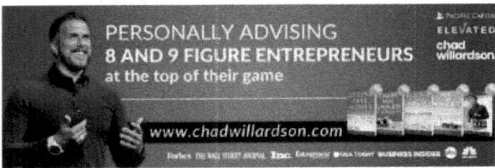

PERSONALLY ADVISING
8 AND 9 FIGURE ENTREPRENEURS
at the top of their game

www.chadwillardson.com

---
* To schedule an appointment with me, please get in touch with my Executive Assistant Oriya directly: oriya@chadwillardson.com

If you're skeptical and wondering if it's unprofessional not to be accessible and available 24/7, or if it risks missing out on opportunities, consider this: Does the actual doctor answer the phone when you call their office? I would feel nervous to go see a surgeon if they answered the phone or immediately emailed me back throughout the day when they were supposed to be doing surgeries. Why is it different for your business? I expect the surgeon to do surgeries and the wealth manager to focus on the most impactful financial management.

Being fully present starts with being intentional. I've learned that if I'm thinking about the past or the future, I'm missing out on the gifts deserving of today. It requires focus. Focus on how I want to show up for my family and aligning these intentions to the shared experience.

One practice we have is to "make a memory." Here's what this looks like: When we're experiencing something really special together, one of us will pause and shout, "Make a memory!" We pause, take a mental picture of the exact moment (the sensory—sight, hearing, smell, taste, and touch). It's so much more powerful than any iPhone picture, as it's capturing an intentional moment and experience in a much more holistic way. Later, when we tell stories, it's so much more colorful and impactful!

When I make this a priority, we live in more alignment with the fruit of the Spirit, experiencing more love, joy, peace, patience, kindness, goodness, faithfulness, gentleness, and with more self-control. Our lives are full and supportive of one another.

**–KELLY KNIGHT,
INTEGRATOR AT EOS® WORLDWIDE**

THE FAMILY DIVIDENDS OF PRESENCE

When you're engaging with your kids or watching their activities, put your phone down. I can tell you from experience that action makes all the difference.

The *only* time I have my phone out at my kids' games is when I'm recording their plays. There's no point in attending an event for your child if you're lost in your screen, with your attention somewhere else, writing texts and reading emails. Trust me, they notice.

My kids recognize and appreciate my presence. They've told me that they love it when I'm at their games because I'm always watching them play, and they can look to me for encouragement or feedback at any time during the game. Because I pay close attention, afterward I can praise what they did great and give them pointers on what to try differently in the future.

It would be easy to be the dad who's just sitting there on his laptop in the bleachers, but that's not being Fully Invested. I've probably attended more than three thousand games for my kids over the years (with at least three thousand more to go), watching them from when they were little all the way to the college level.

I'm proud to be present, watching the game and noticing the nuances of the coaching and team dynamics. Of course, not every parent has the luxury of watching their kids play on the weekend, but for me, that feels like a missed opportunity to deepen my connection with my kids.

*Amber and Chad at Santiago High School California
playoffs supporting Pierce, 2025*

I love getting a look from our kids after they make a great play or even after they get subbed out and go to the bench, because every time we make eye contact, it reinforces to them, "Hey, I'm here for you. You're doing great." I've seen kids look into the stands to see their parents' reaction, and when they realize the parent is not paying attention, they're noticeably bummed out. Similarly, when our kids want attention at home, my wife and I strive to be present and available. I've learned that kids don't really say, "I'm struggling and I need help." Instead, they say something like, "Hey, Dad, will you play with me?"

That's another reason we stopped giving many presents for birthdays or Christmas and instead switched to activities of their choice. We exist in an age of constant distractions right at our fingertips, which is different from when we grew up. Consider the cost of distraction in your home. During the summertime, we pack away the kids' laptops (mostly used for schoolwork anyway) and expect everyone to be outside and more present together. If your kids are under fourteen, you'd be smart to figure out some digital device boundaries sooner rather than later. A recent study shows that receiving a smartphone before age thirteen is associated with poorer mental health outcomes in young adulthood, including suicidal thoughts, detachment from reality, poorer emotional regulation, and diminished self-worth.[9]

Which is why, as you know, our family rule is you don't get a smartphone until age sixteen (and even then, it's regulated with time restrictions and social media access). You may not have those same rules in your home, but the rule itself isn't the point. The point is to prioritize presence fully, even if it's unpopular or uncomfortable. It will pay off in spades.

Strong relationships aren't accidental; they're built on honesty, humility, and the habit of showing up. I want my kids to know that love and loyalty grow when you serve others without keeping score, choose forgiveness over pride, and value connection more than being right. You can't build lasting relationships with your head down, focused only on your own goals. Lift your eyes. Be on the lookout for how to help those around you.

**–KELLY PRICE,
CHAIRMAN OF THE BOARD, CHANGING LIVES FOUNDATION**

PRESENCE IS NONNEGOTIABLE

To be present in my marriage, my wife and I show up for each other as much as we can. In her case, she loves to do extreme races, like half-Ironmans, Tough Mudder races, 29029 Everesting hikes, and even a recent "Escape from Alcatraz" triathlon where she swam in the choppy, cold, shark-infested ocean water near San Francisco. I love going to her races to support her. These events often start between 4:45 a.m. and 5:45 a.m., so attending them and being at the starting line takes commitment! I cheer her on and run around to different places on the course to get videos and give her support. I get emotional every time I see her do her races. Even though I'm just her cheerleader, I feel Fully Invested.

When we traveled for one of her races recently, I'd been super sick in bed for the previous eighteen hours. We were staying at a hotel, and she kissed me goodbye and left at 3:30 in the morning, figuring I wouldn't attend. However, I rallied myself out of bed and found a way to get there before the race started. I was worn down, and it was a thirty-minute drive away from our hotel. But my presence was nonnegotiable. One way or another, I was going to show up.

Amber doing her half-Ironmans

Similarly, she shows up to my ELEVATED live events at the beach and many of my out-of-state speaking engagements. I'm always way more excited to be speaking on stage when I know she's in the crowd supporting me. Being a Fully Invested leader means being present all the time, not just when it's easy. *Especially* when things are hard, you need to show up with presence. My wife and I have been married for twenty-four years, and it's not always smooth sailing. We have plenty of arguments and disagreements, but we continue to deepen and strengthen our connection by showing up for each other.

Chad, Bentley, Pierce, Amber, McKinley, Sterling, and Beckham supporting Amber on Mother's Day after another PR at a Half-Ironman in Panama City, FL.

Presence looks like giving each other the attention when one of us has something important happening. It also looks like regularly scheduled date nights. We have connecting conversations, talking about the week ahead and what's happening. It looks like putting the phone down when you're talking to each other.

We don't always get all of those elements right, but we're conscious of them and follow them more now than in the past. Consistency really does create momentum.

If your spouse or significant other doesn't have you as their most excited cheerleader and supporter, then who will it be? If they can't come home or call you and tell you the exciting news that means a lot to them, who will they call? If something isn't exciting to me, but it's exciting to Amber (like all of her races), then I'm still Fully Invested. I want her to turn to me first and share what she's excited or even nervous about. Make sure you're the first call your significant other makes when they have exciting news to share.

MAKING FAMILY A PRIORITY

Unfortunately, I know a few entrepreneurs who care more about their business associates and contacts than they do their own kids. Obviously, we take care of our clients and do what they hire us to do, but no one should make money at the expense of completely neglecting the relationship with their kids. For example, I was on an important Zoom call recently, and my 10-year-old son Beckham came running into the room to excitedly show me his new braces! I jumped up and gave him high fives and told him how cool it looked. That was a moment when he really wanted to share something important with me. What would happen to his young, tender heart if I yelled at him to get out of the room because I was on a business call? And how would the others on the call react seeing me treat my own son like that? I'm a dad first and a real human being, so anyone I'm doing business with or on the phone with will need to understand that.

Too often, entrepreneurs focus only on what their clients or potential clients want, with no thought to what their families need. Your kids will only love their family if you're showing up for them. And that love is important to me.

My grandparents and parents made family a priority, and that's a legacy we really want to carry on. One thing we consistently follow through on is having weekly family nights together. Sometimes we take Sunday evening walks as a family. We gather together for prayer and devotionals. We take a few family vacations together each year. We show up for each other's sporting events. We strive to have as many family dinners together as possible each week. At Sunday dinner, we talk about the week ahead and what everyone is looking forward to or needs help with. Once again, we are not a perfect family. However, we stay more connected than we otherwise would because of these traditions and habits.

The Willardson Family (minus McKinley) at Balboa Pier, 2025

My wife and I don't have everything figured out, but we've been striving to create a strong family bond from the beginning. We married at twenty-two and twenty and now have five kids, so we basically grew up together. When you're present for your family, they can see that you care and you're not only focused on work. In our family, lots of those connections happen when I'm at their school assembly, their games and practices, my wife's races, kids' recitals, and so on.

If you want to have a strong connection, you have to show up, and showing up is a choice. Over and over. It's not about 100 percent attendance; it's about being fully invested and doing the best you can. We have our share of conflict and struggles (until our oldest turned twenty, we had three teenagers at one time), but our values, traditions, and habits keep us together and strong when times are hardest.

We get to be married, grow a business together, and raise our four kids together. It was clear to us that the growth we were seeking for our firm was never going to be a "win" if our family and marriage suffered as a result. We have zero desire to raise latchkey kids with parents who are only half-present. For us, parenting is a balance between regular and consistent times with our kids—both together and individual time—where they get our undivided attention and family adventure time. It seems that in those adventures—whether small or large—we get to challenge, encourage, and grow together. These "adventure" moments are good material for making "together" memories that stick.

A high-value upgrade we recently instituted is kid date nights at home, where one kid stays up a bit later with Mom and Dad to just play a board game, talk, or snuggle—whatever that kid wants for the evening. They get undivided, individual attention from both parents, which seldom happens naturally. These are moments that deepen our relationship with each one of our kids.

We have also invited our kids into our companies' goals, as if they were also stakeholders in the outcome. They know what target we are looking to achieve, and they know there is a beautiful vacation waiting for them once we reach that goal. We're in it together.

–JEREMIAH LEE,
JD, CFP® AND LAURA LEE, MBA, CFP®
PRINCIPALS, TRICORD ADVISORS

PRESENCE IN BUSINESS

Don't get sucked into the "shiny object syndrome" as an entrepreneur. Your team members, clients, and potential clients can tell if they matter to you. In business, you will actually be judged on your ability to listen and understand what others want. Often, they'll make the decision about whether to work with you based on how present you are in your conversations with them.

> *Don't get sucked into the "shiny object syndrome" as an entrepreneur.*

Someone I used to work with at Merrill Lynch lost a big client because multiple times in the meeting, he looked at his watch and looked out the window while the client was telling a story. It made him seem disinterested, impatient, and unempathetic. The client was so insulted that they took their multimillion-dollar account elsewhere. That was a great lesson for me to witness.

When you're in the growth phase of your business, how do you know what's worth your attention and presence? Here's one way to handle it: I have an assistant strictly filter my meeting requests because early on, I too often agreed to meetings and gave my attention freely to people who didn't align with my business goals. I'd get into a meeting and realize they were just trying to sell me a program or raise investment money for *their* new idea, even though they said they wanted to talk about something else. I've learned the hard way to better filter opportunities fully worth my time and attention. By saying no to meetings and appointments that don't serve your future, you create more intentional space for those who deserve your attention: your existing team members and clients.

Our ELEVATED Team in Dana Point, 2025

A Fully Invested leader has genuine relationships with people on their business team, and the people on the business team feel understood and cared for because of the presence of their Fully Invested leader.

When you communicate with the people who work for you or with you, put your phone away and make eye contact so they know that you're listening. Train people on the power of focus, single-tasking, time blocking, batching activities, doing one thing at a time, and reducing their notifications. Everything that helps *you* be Fully Invested will also help the productivity and cohesion of your team.

I've always believed that the key to moving a team from "somewhat committed" to "fully invested" is creating a culture where they feel ownership, purpose, and connection. For me, it's about empowering my team to think like entrepreneurs within the company, giving them the freedom to innovate, the responsibility to lead, and the rewards that come with delivering results. When people feel like they're building something bigger than themselves, they show up differently. Our team doesn't just work for the company; they work with it, and that alignment has driven loyalty, creativity, and a place people are proud to be a part of.

–DEAN GRAZIOSI,
ENTREPRENEUR AND NEW YORK TIMES BESTSELLING AUTHOR

Chad with friends Dean Graziosi and Lewis Howes

DON'T WAIT

I once had a client who worked in the roofing industry. He was obsessed with getting his financial accounts and net account balance up to $40 million. It was an arbitrary number, but to him, it symbolized security and having "made it." He let that number drive him to the point that he worked nearly every waking hour, seven days a week, for twenty years.

> *Fully Invested leaders know that great long-term investments compound over time, and successful investing requires consistency, patience, discipline, and time.*

He missed both of his kids' entire childhoods. Now they're in their twenties, and he's trying to buy their love after having neglected them. It's not working well, and he frequently expresses regrets about being an absentee husband (now divorced) and absentee dad. When it comes to investing in anything—relationships or financial accounts—you can't make up for lost time. Fully Invested leaders know that great long-term investments compound over time, and successful investing requires consistency, patience, discipline, and time.

Think of it like planting a tree. If you want the vast shade of a mature, thirty-year-old tree, you can't wait for twenty-nine years, finally plant the seed, and then catch up by giving it ten times as much water. Deeply rooted growth—real growth—doesn't work that way.

The same goes for your family relationships. If you think you can grind for a decade now and care about your family later, after you've "made it," you're on a path to wake up one day with terrible regrets. Like that roofer client. A Fully Invested leader doesn't put off what they want most for what they want now. Always keep sight of your vision and mission, and choose how to use your time accordingly.

When we married, we were super young and super broke. We haven't struggled financially much over the past fifteen years, but we still have our fair share of challenges, from parenting our five busy kids to the stress of entrepreneurship. What's really made a difference for us in this nearly quarter-century of marriage is all the invested time and effort in our relationship.

McKinley, Sterling, Chad, Baby Beckham, Amber, Bentley, and Pierce, 2015

Conventional wisdom tells you to give the bulk of your time, energy, and attention to earning more money before you start a family. You're told that you can't start a family without financial security first. We just never accepted that idea and felt that we could figure out ways to get by and that eventually the investment in our young family and future would pay dividends. It's too common to think you can find a neat and tidy "balance" (which doesn't exist) or that you can neglect your family to build your career, but that's an expensive trade-off that comes with consequences later.

If you haven't been Fully Invested in both your business career and your family, don't beat yourself up. Let's get to work on changing that, starting today.

FULLY INVESTED FRAMEWORK: PRESENCE

Centering gratitude can make all the difference, especially when it comes to presence. Use this worksheet to reflect and guide you.

_ PRESENCE THROUGH GRATITUDE™

ELEVATED
FULLY INVESTED™

GROWTH	
What challenge shaped you into who you are now?	What do you now appreciate more?

RELATIONSHIPS	
Who showed up for you this year - how can you thank them?	Who challenges you to grow, and why are you grateful for them?

MOMENTS	
What simple moment reminded you why you do this?	When did you last slow down and truly feel present?

CHOOSE GRATITUDE. IT CHANGES EVERYTHING.

For a downloadable version of this worksheet and other resources, scan the QR code below.

CHALLENGE: THE 10-MINUTE CONNECTION RULE[IP]

Purpose: If you want to strengthen a relationship, whether with an employee, a co-worker, a spouse, a client, or a child, this simple daily habit will pay off 10X (and then some).

Spend at least ten minutes daily fully present with someone important. No distractions. Just engaged conversation.

- At work: Check in with a key team member. Ask about their challenges, ideas, and vision.
- At home: Have a device-free conversation with your spouse or kids—one that makes them feel heard and valued.

Why It Works: The best leaders aren't the ones who talk the most; they're the ones who listen the best.

KEY TAKEAWAYS

▸ At the end of the day, your team doesn't need more emails; they need clarity. Your family doesn't need more gifts or trips; they need your attention and presence.

▸ Multitasking is a lie. Your brain can only do one important thing at a time.

▸ The conventional way of navigating the world is a trap. Most people don't control their attention. They react to everything—endless notifications, low-value conversations, social media, rabbit holes, and other people's problems. Fully Invested leaders eliminate distractions, refuse unnecessary meetings, and turn off notifications. You can have an amazing day outside the inbox.

▸ If you want to have a strong connection, you have to show up—and showing up is a choice. Over and over. It's not about perfection; it's about full investment.

▸ When it comes to investing in anything—relationships, your financial accounts—you can't make up for lost time. Investments compound over time, and successful investing requires consistency, patience, discipline, and time.

CHAPTER 7

Build Championship Teams

Do you remember the iconic Chicago Bulls team of the nineties? Or the dynasty of the Lakers with Shaq and Kobe?

Of course you do. A better question is probably who *doesn't* remember those lineups. Those teams didn't win championships just because of star players—they won because they built a high-performance ecosystem under Phil Jackson's leadership, one that could sustain greatness over time. Before Coach Jackson came on board, Jordan dominated, but the Bulls kept losing in the playoffs. Jackson introduced the triangle offense, a system that distributed responsibility across the team. And when Jordan trusted his teammates, they became unstoppable. The truth is that championship teams aren't made of five Michael Jordans or five Kobe Bryants. They succeed because each person embraces their specific role at an elite level. I was fortunate enough to personally meet them both (see below).

Chad and Michael Jordan

Chad and Kobe Bryant (RIP); McKinley Willardson and Gigi Bryant (RIP)

Scottie Pippen was the ultimate number two—unselfish, defensive genius, playmaker. Dennis Rodman didn't care about scoring—he became a rebounding machine and defensive beast. He once had a game with zero points and twenty-eight rebounds. Don't forget Steve Kerr, their three-point specialist. As for the Lakers, Shaq and Kobe learned (at least for their three championships together) that their roles were different, but equally important.

And Phil Jackson wasn't just a coach—he was a master of human psychology. He wasn't obsessed with X's and O's—he was obsessed with chemistry, leadership, and self-mastery. He coached egos while keeping the team united. He didn't micromanage—he often let players figure things out on the court instead of always calling timeouts. Coach Jackson learned about each player's background and got to know their natural tendencies and interests, even off the court. He inspired players to buy into a larger philosophy by introducing focus, self-awareness, meditation, Zen, and mindfulness to keep them calm under pressure. And boy, did it work.

What can we learn from these championship dynasties? That pressure isn't the enemy; it's the proving ground. That's where your team (or family) can create a culture of chemistry, despite their differences. That's where personal accountability and frequent communication matter a lot. A Fully Invested leader will ensure that even when there are challenges or struggles, the team is unified in solving them, more focused on getting it right than on *being* right.

Pressure isn't the enemy; it's the proving ground.

How did Phil Jackson do it? Well, he got the best out of each player by helping them expand on who they were instead of focusing on who they were not. He saw them for their greatness within and asked, *"How can I get the best out of that person in service of the overall team?"* That's why he's considered one of the winningest coaches (coached NBA teams to eleven championship wins) of all time in all sports.

Jackson used Zen to channel focus, purpose, clarity, peace under stress, and calmness in the face of chaos. He knew how to work on the inner game first and not let all the outside energy affect him or his players. I strive to bring a similar philosophy to our businesses, team members, and clients. Helping our Pacific Capital clients remain Fully Invested despite volatile financial markets and recessions makes all the difference in their long-term results.

It's important not to overreact when the ocean gets choppy. Usually, when coaches see their team struggling and falling behind, they get frantic and worried and call a timeout. Phil Jackson was the exception. He almost never stopped the action in those moments. Instead, he'd let his teams battle through the difficulty and figure out how to mentally bounce back.

There were so many times when the Bulls or Lakers were spiraling downward in a game, and fans would be frantically upset, urging him to call a timeout, but he'd stay calm and leave it to the players to get themselves out of trouble. That way, by the time they reached the playoffs, they were battle-tested and confident that they could turn things around mentally, rather than slouching on the bench feeling defeated and waiting to be told how to fix it. He cultivated self-reliant players with the resilience of a championship mindset.

For business teams, it's also important to teach self-reliance and resilience. As a Fully Invested leader, you want to find people with complementary strengths, lead them with vision, help them own their results towards serving your customers and clients. Of course, you don't want to let them drown and fail on your dime or at the expense of losing business, but you can lead them and give them as much independence as possible so they can grow and thrive in their respective roles.

LA Rams Super Bowl Champion Coach Sean McVay and Chad

One of the most important roles of a leader is to be a vision-ary. This is key and critical for creating clarity of where we are headed and how we're going to get there through action-able steps. To get the buy-in and excitement, people must know the intent and purpose of the vision and how their role is vital to making it come to fruition. Any great vision has shared ownership and an understanding of how everyone's roles contribute to the goal of the team.

After that, one of the best ways we encourage our team to lean into pressure and not shy away from it is through storytell-ing and previous examples of real growth occurring through those experiences, both positive and negative. You don't grow through it unless you go through it and lean into the reward-ing challenge of doing hard things, truly attacking success, and not fearing failure. Have a growth mindset through it all.

–SEAN MCVAY,
LA RAMS COACH

EQUAL ISN'T THE SAME

Let's take a look at the role of championship teams on the home front. Sometimes the world makes it seem like a husband and wife have identical roles, but they don't. Before you get sensitive regarding what I'm about to say, hear me out: If two people have the exact same role, one of them is not necessary. If two people think alike, one of them is not necessary. That's a widely accepted concept for business partnerships. You must bring complementary skill sets to the partnership.

In other words, you and your spouse better have different roles that complement each other. Figure out what your natural strengths are and understand that you're equal, but different.

Amber and Chad, Balboa Bay, 2022

I mentioned this before, but it's worth saying again: many people think they and their spouse should each do 50 percent of every job so it's "fair," but that doesn't make any sense. When our first child was born, my wife quit her job to stay home and take care of our baby girl. And since we both came from big families and wanted that same fun environment, we had four additional kids over the next eleven years. We envisioned a partnership where I would provide and protect, and she would care for and nurture the family and home. Both are important and equal roles, but very different. It would be a poor use of our resources and time if we insisted on each doing 50 percent of each other's roles.

I recognize that our family dynamics might be different from yours, but this is what we wanted, and it works great for us. Regardless of whatever you feel about gender stereotypes or your own family duties, you have to give 100 percent to whatever your role is. Be Fully Invested in your family role in your current phase of life. That role might change over time. The important part is that *equal* does not mean *the same*. In my marriage, we've figured out that we can have different roles and still be 100 percent equal. There's nothing that's lower or higher, worse or better. At any given phase, we figure out what each of us needs to do to contribute fully to the family, while recognizing that those needs shift over time.

> *Be Fully Invested in your family role in your current phase of life.*

Funny, but true: when mechanical or maintenance people come to our house and knock on the door, for instance, they ask for me (because they expect the husband to be the handyman and not the wife), but they should ask for Amber. I don't know how to fix anything and am not good with tools, whereas she knows how stuff works and really enjoys fixing things. If the poor guy is explaining something that needs to be done with the pipes, I understand none of it, while she understands all of it. Thankfully, her strengths make up for my weaknesses. If someone's coming to negotiate the cost of a job, Amber doesn't want to talk about the money, so that's my responsibility. Or when Amber is asked to give a speech or a presentation, she leans on me to help her prepare it and make sure she's ready to succeed because that comes naturally to me.

Putting people in a box and saying everything is fifty-fifty doesn't work in real life. Part of keeping your marriage strong is learning your relative strengths and interests, getting comfortable with your roles, taking accountability, and, maybe most importantly, appreciating what your partner brings to the relationship. If you think about it, appreciation in both the financial and the relationship senses translates to an increase in value. So think about how you can appreciate and value each other's strengths more and give 100 percent effort in your contribution.

Healthy relationships start with us. They start with self-love. That's why, even for my baby girl, who is five months old, I try to drill these mantras into her subconscious:

I love myself.

I honor myself.

I respect myself.

Now, a relationship between two people is like anything else in the world: it takes work, understanding, and evolution. Commitment is different than just a temporary feeling. And if you want to commit, there has to be a shared goal, shared purpose, shared mission, and shared values. If not, eventually the energy will fade away. I would advise not only to look for "who" is right, but also to look for alignment in terms of values and direction of life.

—DR. EHAB HAMARNEH,
FOUNDER OF BE YOU

BUILD YOUR TEAM AROUND YOUR CLIENTS

Championship teams are vital at work too. Within the wealth advisory industry, it's common for firms to grow by recruiting and hiring many financial advisors and wealth managers. In this model, advisors essentially run their own "practice" and service their own clients, which creates siloed businesses within the business. A company might have twenty different advisors, and each client is a client of a specific advisor. The resulting system has twenty different investment philosophies, processes, types of clients, and even fee rates. That model lacks cohesion and increases competition amongst advisors from within the firm, competing for deals, competing for the attention of shared service team members. With nearly a quarter-century in the wealth management industry, I've seen the downside to that growth model. While it helps the firm grow at a faster pace, it does not benefit the clients of the firm.

By contrast, I've designed Pacific Capital to be one team of experts, each contributing a different skill set to the client experience.

Every client is a client of Pacific Capital as a whole. There are no competing advisors or sales reps, and no one who works here earns any commissions. If someone seeks to hire us, that person is a client of the whole firm, and everyone knows who they are. If they have a question, they can ask anyone. Everyone on the team has their own highly specific role based on their niche expertise, and we serve only one type of client: high-net-worth entrepreneurs.

My vision for creating Pacific Capital like this was to surround the client with a team of experts who serve the client's needs. Our clients appreciate knowing that they have access to the entire team and can work with whoever has the expertise in their particular area of need.

Once I left Merrill Lynch in 2011, I wanted to put entrepreneurial clients at the forefront and figure out everything that they needed. Then I hired experts based on those needs. The more we learn about what our clients want, the faster we can add quality talent and expertise to fill that need. Similarly, in ELEVATED (our accountability mastermind community), every team member is an expert in their own arena to serve our entrepreneur members— whether through masterminds, one-on-one coaching, or other communication—but they all work together for the members. At Pacific Capital, the whole team is built to serve the individual clients of the ELEVATED community.

Chad and Ninad Tipnis (JTCPL Designs), Pacific Capital headquarters

Centering the client is an industry-agnostic approach for business success. Whoever you serve, put them at the center and then build your team outward from there. Don't assemble a team that serves the business and then try to cram new clients and customers into the mix. Build your business team around your clients' needs first.

THE VALUE OF CLEAR COMMUNICATION AND EXPECTATIONS

Fully Invested leaders are not afraid to have difficult and direct conversations. Tim Ferris famously said, "A person's success in life can usually be measured by the number of uncomfortable conversations he or she is willing to have."[10] This approach applies across the board, both at work and at home. It's about mutual exchange, active listening, and understanding with an intention to move forward together. A Fully Invested leader doesn't hide from challenges or conflict. Nor are they a bully or a tyrant. Instead, they focus on how to work through challenges, resolve concerns, how to support and encourage their people

For all my businesses, I meet with all my team members and coach them individually. We talk about how things are going, what needs to get better, and set clear expectations. This begins from before they're even hired. The ELEVATE AND THRIVE resource I shared in chapter 5 (see p. 117) can also help you clarify role expectations in your organization. Taking this extra time up front to set clear expectations for anyone you work with might feel like just another task, but it's so much more than that. Unclear expectations are the source of conflict, failure, and disappointment.

Clarity is kindness. Whether at home or at work, I've learned that most friction comes from unspoken expectations. I try to make the invisible visible, stating what I need, what I'm committing to, and what success looks like.

At work, that means defining outcomes and ownership up front. At home, it means checking in emotionally, not just logistically. The goal is the same in both places: alignment, trust, and fewer surprises.

–LIOR WEINSTEIN,
FOUNDER, CTOX.COM

CENTER TEAMS, NOT EGOS

Superstars don't win championships alone. Teams do. Remember that Michael Jordan was the best player on the planet, but he wasn't a champion until he learned how to trust the team. The same is true for all the greats in team sports. Chemistry and teamwork are greater than talent. There's no "I" in "team." Championship teams don't fear pressure; they crave it.

If you have to do everything yourself and your way and you surround yourself with order-takers, you don't have a team; you have a supporting cast for your ego. Sadly, that's what many entrepreneurs actually want. It goes back to the illusion of busyness as a badge of honor. That's one reason I didn't name my wealth management firm something like "Willardson & Associates," which would have subordinated the team. If I centered myself in my business, then clients would be disappointed if they called and didn't talk to Willardson, but rather to "only" an associate. Instead, I center the client and emphasize the power and abilities of our team.

Dane and I have always shared the same goals for our family, guided by the gospel of Jesus Christ. While we have different parenting styles, the objectives are always aligned.

In this new phase of life, where our children are responsible for themselves, we still are very united in supporting their growth and development, while also supporting each other's interests and efforts in exploring new ventures and goals.

Sometimes we have differences of opinion about HOW to progress, but never about whether TO progress or why. I think because we trust each other's motivations and overall intentions, we know we can figure out the "how."

−WENDY KIMBER,
LIFE COACH AND FOUNDER OF WENDY KIMBER COACHING

FULLY INVESTED FRAMEWORKS: CHAMPIONSHIP TEAMS

F.A.M.I.L.Y.

You've taken an important step toward solving the biggest challenge most ambitious entrepreneurs face: how to build a thriving business *without* sacrificing precious time with your family. And, as you may have guessed, I've got a system for that: the F.A.M.I.L.Y. Framework.[IP]

F - FAMILY DINNERS

We have five kids who all play at least two sports.

Everyone is busy.

There are countless reasons why we "shouldn't" have time for family dinner, but we make it happen four or five out of seven days!

Sometimes we eat at 4 p.m., sometimes at 8:45 p.m., but we prioritize it because research shows that children who have regular family meals have better mental and physical health, along with stronger relationships with parents. Also, 80 percent of teenagers say they're more willing to open up and share their struggles during family mealtime, and 60 percent of children have lower suicidal tendencies when they have regular meals at home with their family.[11] Sadly, less than one in four families sit down to eat together. Not because they don't want to, but because they're exhausted, busy, distracted, and overwhelmed by the daily grind.

Once we sit down at the table, we follow these four family standards:

- Rule #1 - No cell phones at the dinner table (except for a quick family mealtime photo)
- Rule #2 - Everyone shares their high and low for the day
- Rule #3 - Round table setup so there's no "head," giving everyone an equal voice
- Rule #4 - Open discussion time where we can ask anything (stuff they heard about at school, challenges with friends, goals for an upcoming game, stress about a test, what mom and dad are scared of, funny jokes, etc.)

If you do it consistently, dinnertime becomes peaceful instead of rushed, kids are more willing to help in the kitchen, and the chaos that used to rule your evenings melts away. You see, the "secret" to being present and invested in your kid's life isn't about having the perfect schedule; it's about creating a consistent space where real connection happens. And there's no better place than the dinner table!

A - AFFIRMATIONS AND AFFECTION

A strong family learns to communicate by affirming their own identity, affirming each other, and showing affection. It could be done in different ways, but here's how we do it:

Way 1: Affirmations:

Our kids have their own "I Am" statements on a poster board in their bedroom.

It doesn't matter if they're six or twenty years old...

They recite their "I Am" statements every day. Before they go to bed *and* in the morning, they read them out loud.

- "I am successful."
- "I am confident."
- "I am powerful."
- "I am strong."
- "I am kind."
- "I am getting better and better every day."

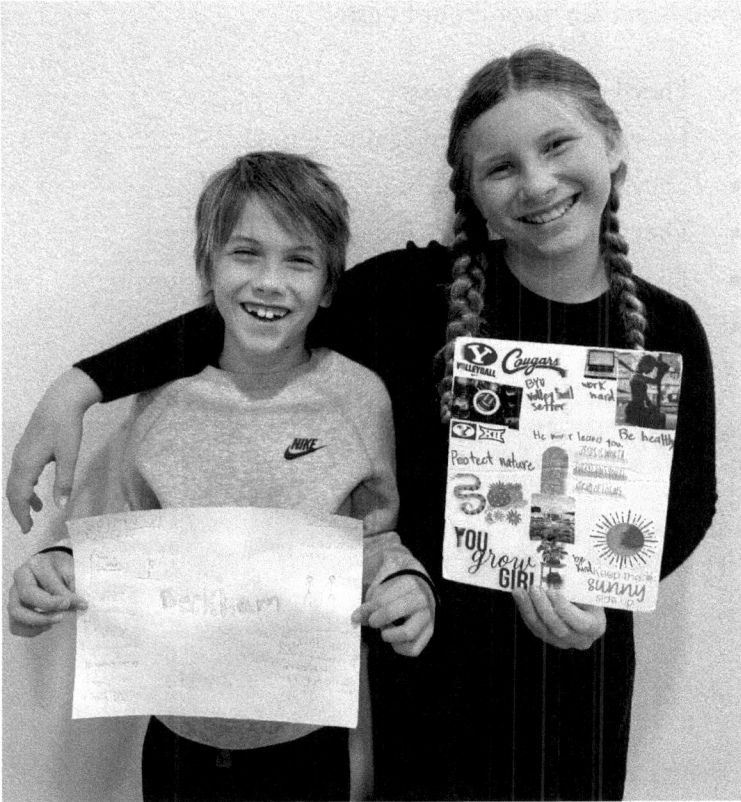

Beckham and Bentley with "I AM" statements and Vision Boards

Way 2: Affection

Our family has established non-negotiable moments of connection:

- Hugs when leaving the house
- Hugs when returning home
- Physical affection, even during conflicts
- Hugs before bedtime

Here are some fun facts about hugs:

- They help reduce stress.
- They may protect you against illness.
- They may boost your heart health.
- They can reduce fears and anxiety.
- They can make you happier and boost oxytocin.
- They help you communicate.

Sterling, Beckham, and Pierce, Balboa Pier, California, 2025

Family therapist Virginia Satir once said, "We need four hugs a day for survival. We need 8 hugs a day for maintenance. We need 12 hugs a day for growth."[12] I grew up in a family that hugs. When I first met my in-laws, they weren't affectionate at all. My father-in-law's arms stayed stiff at his sides during hugs, and he seemed like he didn't know what to do when I went in for the big bear hug (as a new son-in-law). But over time, this culture of affection has definitely spread throughout much of my in-laws' family. Whether through physical touch or acts of service, showing affection builds bonds that withstand life's challenges.

M - MEANINGFUL TRADITIONS

Studies show that family security and strength come from consistency and structure. Children thrive when they have traditions to look forward to. One of the traditions we have comes every October when we dress up in themed costumes together as a family on Halloween. Here are a few of our favorites in the recent past:

Batman theme

Alice in Wonderland

Space

Star Wars

The Wizard of Oz

Zookeepers

The cool part about this tradition is that Amber and I aren't the ones deciding on the costume themes—*everybody* is. And everybody has a chance to present their own ideas. Our kids have even made PowerPoint presentations pitching their theme ideas starting in early summer. Then we vote as a family and begin gathering costumes and accessories.

It would be easier to let our older teenagers skip this tradition, dress up as "something cool," and hang with friends at a high school Halloween party that night. But that's just not what we do. They have space to hang out with their high school friends and celebrate that week, but Halloween night is reserved for our family tradition of dressing up for a family theme and walking our neighborhood together. And we love that our older kids willingly participate.

I - INSPIRING VISION

Every member of our family, even the littlest ones, participates in our annual vision board ritual at the kitchen table. This takes place sometime during the last week of each year and lasts at least a few hours.

Family Vision Board Annual Tradition

We categorize dreams into multiple areas of life, using magazines and other visuals to make these dreams tangible. I'll never forget when McKinley, at age eight or nine, cut out the word *college* from a magazine and a basketball player, declaring she wanted to play college basketball. She didn't even know how to play yet! But that vision and dedicated work led to multiple scholarship offers by age eighteen and eventually a spot on the BYU Women's Basketball team.

Another ambitious goal was one my wife wrote on her vision board. At the time, the farthest she'd ever run in a race was a community 5k. But on her board, she wrote that she'd compete in a half-ironman. She cut out pictures of a female cyclist, a female swimmer, and a female runner. I'm happy to report that not only has she completed many half-Ironmans since that vision board, but she's done marathons and other extreme races as well! And she keeps getting new PRs at every event.

And then there's our son Pierce, who set four big volleyball goals this season that were all reflected on his vision board: go 10–0 and win the league championship, earn an MVP award, break three all-time school records, and win the Southern California Championship. Attending a large high school of 3,600+ students with 31 years of sports history and many D1 volleyball players, even achieving one of those four goals, would be a big deal. But guess what? The career block record at his high school was 127, and he finished with 263. He led his team to win the Southern California Regional Championship and finished Top 20 in the country for blocks and kills. Amber and I were beyond impressed by him, not just meeting but exceeding his ambitious goals.

Is this luck? Nope! These kinds of accomplishments come to fruition after a lot of hard work, and they all begin with your family's vision of your future. If you're great at inspiring vision in your business, you must bring that same energy home to your family! This works for young children and adult children, too. I plan to continue this tradition with future grandchildren.

Amber breaking her own record in the Mexico City Half-Ironman, 2025

L - LOVE AND GRATITUDE

As a faith-based family, we believe gratitude requires some sacrifice. For example, we've made handwritten thank-you cards a part of what we do. If our kids have a birthday party with twenty friends bringing gifts, they write twenty thank-you cards before playing with those presents. Our ten-year-old son, Beckham, spent a long time today writing thank-yous to all of his birthday guests who recently came over to his swim party. Our eighteen-year-old son, Pierce, recently spent a few hours writing thank-you cards to all the people who sent him money as a congratulations for graduating high school. This isn't a chore for them—it's how we build a culture of appreciation in our family.

> *Gratitude opens doors of opportunity.*

That's the kind of mindset we want our kids to have because gratitude is part of who we are. Have you ever noticed that you can't be grateful and angry at the same time? Gratitude opens doors of opportunity. In this fast-paced world, genuine gratitude really stands out. By the way, learning how to appreciate what you have also prevents one of the top killers of success and wealth-building: an attitude of entitlement (if you haven't yet read my second book, *Smart, Not Spoiled*, check it out). We're programming our kids' minds to see abundance through the lens of gratitude. This shifts their entire worldview from:

"What do I get?" to

"What can I give?"

Chad and Amber, Park City, Utah, Valentine's Day, 2019

Y - YIELDING SERVICE

We actively build a culture of service through:

- Service trips and camps
- Volunteer missions
- Dedicated service days during vacations

One of my proudest Dad moments was during our first family vacation in the Bahamas many years back. We stayed at the famous Atlantis resort. We spent part of our first day at an orphanage. I still remember the taxi driver's confusion when he picked us up from the all-inclusive waterslide resort on the beach and took us to an inner city orphanage, far from the fun and touristy beaches. The unforgettable moment was on our last free day of the trip. Our kids could choose to do anything at that resort, like waterslides, the beach, or jet skis, but they unanimously wanted to return to the orphanage to play with those children again. They felt that inner joy from serving someone in need, and it felt more important than simply doing something "fun." That's what happens when service becomes part of your family DNA. You absolutely will change your family's direction when you make serving others part of who you are, not just something you do.

An Eagle Scout himself, Chad has continued in scouting, serving as Scout Master and Regional Leader for many years

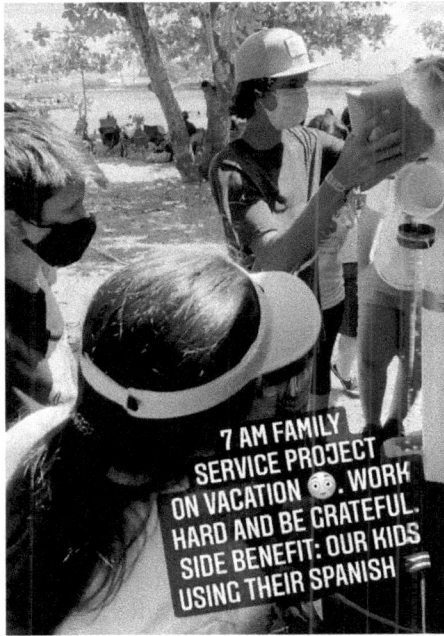

Willardson family beach cleanup at 6:00 a.m. in Puerto Rico, 2020

Pierce doing construction on a three-week service trip to Northern India, 2024

CHALLENGE: NO TIME-OUTS

Purpose: If you're the "Michael Jordan" of your business or family, ask yourself, "Am I the bottleneck?" At work and at home, you can create leaders who can handle high-pressure situations without always relying on you.

Step 1: Next time a team or family member faces a challenge, resist the urge to step in immediately.

Step 2: Instead, ask them the following questions:

- What's the best way to handle this?
- What have you already tried?
- What's the next step?

Why It Works: Letting people solve problems on their own isn't just a good tool for building skills and autonomy. If you're like me, you might even find they have a better strategy or solution than the one you had in mind!

KEY TAKEAWAYS

- Pressure isn't the enemy; it's the proving ground where your team (or family) can create a culture of chemistry, despite their differences. It's where personal accountability and frequent communication matter a lot.

- If two people have the exact same role, one of them is not necessary. If two people think exactly alike, one of them is not necessary. That's a widely accepted concept for business partnerships. You must bring complementary skill sets to the partnership.

- Whoever you serve, put them at the center and then build your team outward from there. Don't assemble a team that serves the business and then try to cram new clients and customers into the mix. Build your business team around your clients' needs first.

- If you have to do everything yourself and your way and you surround yourself with order-takers, you don't have a team; you have a supporting cast for your ego.

CHAPTER 8

Choose Your People, Choose Your Path

As my friend Tony Robbins says, "Proximity is power."[13]

Tony Robbins and Chad, Coeur d'Alene Resort, 2025

Proximity really is power because humans calibrate to the room.

Who you're close to sets your standards, speed, and ceiling. You really do adopt the expectations of your tightest circle. If growth and excellence are the default around you, underperformance feels uncomfortable. Your inner circle—your people—shape your identity. Life outcomes are social. Decades of research in network science and behavioral economics show that behaviors (health, financial habits, work effort), beliefs, and even emotions spread through close ties and their friends-of-friends. Your inner circle doesn't just influence what you do; it resets what feels normal.

This matters both in your home life and your business life. For your marriage and family, the tone at home is your most powerful proximity. Gratitude, faith, discipline, and optimism—modeled daily—compound across years and generations. Unequal commitment doesn't endure at home or at work. Your closest people need to be Fully Invested alongside you for love and work to pull in the same direction.

My friend John Ruhlin, author and founder of Giftology, was a fantastic example of choosing people and realizing the power of investing in relationships. He was Fully Invested in the important people in his life. One of the last gifts he gave me before passing away unexpectedly last year was a customized mug at an entrepreneurship conference in Nashville, Tennessee. Below is a picture of him giving me the mug in front of the audience; a month later, sadly, he passed away. This is the last time I saw him. John taught me the power of thoughtful gifting and how you can transform relationships by being a great gift-giver. If you knew John, you knew he loved you by how he treated you and how he gave gifts to people.

Chad and John Rhulin, Gift-o-logy

RELATIONSHIPS THAT LIFT (AND THOSE THAT DON'T)

Early on, after founding Pacific Capital, I hired someone brilliant on paper. At first, they looked Fully Invested. Over time, signs to the contrary appeared: they dismissed teammates' ideas in meetings, began refusing to complete needed work, created conflict with fellow team members, and turned small issues into personal drama. I tried to get clarity, give coaching, and worked on multiple formal improvement plans with him. Nothing changed—because the problem wasn't skill; it was ego.

My mistake was waiting too long to fire him. Our team felt the painful cost before I was willing to cut him loose. A few team members finally said, "We don't want to come to work anymore if he's still here." When I made the change, the energy in our office flipped! Not only that, over the next two years, our business grew by 271 percent! More importantly, high positive energy, unity, teamwork, and trust became the baseline again. Keeping the wrong relationship isn't neutral; it taxes everyone around you who is committed.

Releasing that person wasn't easy. I'd convinced myself they were "too hard to replace." They weren't. You may think you can't afford to let a high producer go, but if they're eroding trust and standards, you can't afford to keep them.

The inverse is just as true. The right fits raise energy—and standards—immediately. For example, my two executive assistants are excellent fits. They've gotten to know my values, preferences, growth mindset, and even my wife and children. They're coachable, proactive, and dependable. I trust them to represent me, to make calls and take meetings on my behalf without hand-holding. One thing I've learned as an entrepreneur is that people don't really leave jobs; they leave leaders (and work environments). Your team can tell if you're genuinely and fully invested in them, and they'll meet you at your level.

This principle also applies at home. Though you don't "fire" a spouse, you do prune behaviors and reinforce standards: respect in conflict, quick repair attempts, shared goals, supportive energy, and consistent follow-through. Home is your closest proximity—its tone multiplies or constrains everything else.

HOW TO APPLY THIS PRINCIPLE

To apply this principle, try the following:

Implement the Decision Rule (use quarterly): Would I enthusiastically rehire this person today? If yes: Invest in them more—clarify a growth path and give more ownership. If no, because of skills: coach with a measurable plan for improvement by a specific date. If no, because of values, ego, or mistrust, plan a clean and fast exit from the business relationship. If you realize this person is not Fully Invested and it's time to move on, use a script like this to make the change: "We're ending the role today because of [specific standards] that haven't changed despite clear timelines and support. We'll support a smooth transition and references aligned to your strengths."

Immediately reset norms with the team: "Standards didn't change—enforcement did. Here's what great looks like. Here's how we'll support you." At the same time, double down on those who are really showing up for you. Continue your one-on-ones and be sure to give recognition for the job well done.

Create a rhythm at home. The way to apply this at home is to really create a rhythm that reinforces your communication and connection as a family. Go over your calendar together weekly and huddle up with your spouse as well. Find ways to get to a "faster repair" after conflict or disagreement (strive to own it and resolve it that day). Set up a monthly date tied to a shared goal or hobby (health, service, faith, or a family project). My wife and I have gotten into pickleball, golf, and padel lately. One of the best dates we've had in a while was last week when we did a private pickleball lesson at the Newport Beach Country Club and then went out to breakfast together. The bottom line is that when you invest in your marriage and family, home becomes a steady tailwind for everything else.

Amber and Chad getting into golf and pickleball together, 2025

I hate to admit it, but I've made my fair share of hiring mistakes, and the most costly ones weren't about bringing someone on too soon or too late. The hardest lesson came from keeping someone on the team far too long. She was hardworking, clients loved her, and I could always rely on her, but she repeatedly made critical thinking mistakes that set us back years. I ignored what I knew deep down: she didn't have the skill set to take our clients—or the agency—to the next level. When I finally made the tough call to let her go, we doubled our revenue and 10X client results almost immediately. That experience changed everything. Now, my golden rule is this: if I'm hiring for a position, the person has to be better at it than I am. I don't need them to share my vision, but they must be able to execute with more depth and precision than I could.

You always hear "hire slow, fire fast," but what's helped me live that out is confronting issues head-on, documenting everything, and letting facts and patterns—not feelings— drive decisions. When someone paints their own picture with missed expectations and data, the decision to part ways becomes clear. And when you've given them every opportunity to grow, you can walk away knowing you led with fairness and clarity.

–DANIELLE SABRINA,
CEO, SOCIETY22 PR

YOUR NETWORK IS YOUR SUPERPOWER

I join coaching groups and masterminds *for the people in the room.*
I want high ambition, abundance mindsets, high character, and a
real love for family. A Fully Invested leader builds with those headed
where they want to go.

There are countless groups out there; the key is finding your people.
As the song "Find Your People" puts it, *"You got to find your people,
then you'll find yourself."*[14] Different rooms have different goals and
cultures; choose the one that matches your standards.

Chad, Nick Sansone, Sean Martin, Andrew Sallee

When I created ELEVATED, I built "the room" I couldn't find elsewhere: leaders who are all-in on winning at work and at home. Not just money and flash; we're talking character, family, and long-term impact. Our distinction is a high-quality network of peers who excel in both arenas and hold each other to that same standard. I believe any network that prioritizes money over meaning leaves you rich in dollars and poor in purpose. If you can't find the right room you're looking for, build it.

The following image is a note from an ELEVATED member who has been with us since its inception. I love that she credits my deep commitment to faith and marriage as the reason for her joining our community, which is a key differentiator between us and other groups!

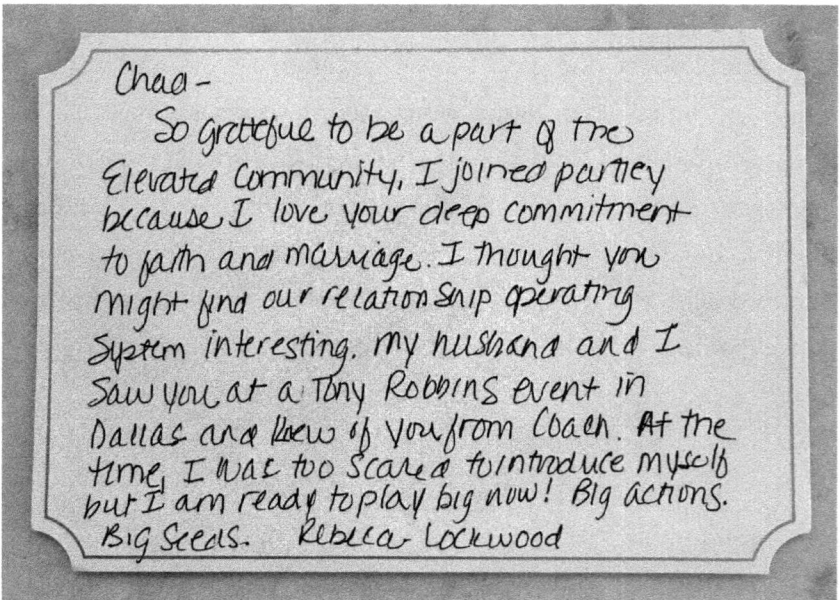

> Chad—
>
> So grateful to be a part of the Elevated Community, I joined partley because I love your deep commitment to faith and marriage. I thought you might find our relationship operating system interesting. My husband and I saw you at a Tony Robbins event in Dallas and knew of you from Coach. At the time, I was too scared to introduce myself but I am ready to play big now! Big actions. Big Seeds. Rebecca Lockwood

CULTIVATING STRONG RELATIONSHIPS

This lesson starts at home.

I tell our five kids the same thing I'll tell you: your friends are your future. You won't see the effect right away, but it compounds. Spend time with five smokers, and you'll be the sixth. Spend time with five marathoners, and you'll start lacing up (I've seen that firsthand with my wife and her Ironman friend groups). We copy the room we're in. Choose the room. Here's a group of moms and daughters after a "MudGirl" race that Amber and our daughter Bentley competed in recently:

Coach your kids to pick friends who lift them up, not drain them. We look for kids who are kind, who speak well of others, who don't mock our beliefs, and who make it easier to live our values. We encourage them to choose peers who are active, aiming for a goal, and not inviting them to cut corners or break rules.

Friends don't need the same goals. They need the same drive—the shared belief that striving matters.

For me, the most important relationships are with God, spouse, and then children, in that order. If you mess up those first three, it's tough to do well in the rest of your life. Everyone and everything else comes *after.*

Having a shared vision in our marriage and home brings clarity, unity, and peace. It means we're not pulling in different directions; we're building the same future together. When my wife, Shawna, and I are aligned, everything flows more smoothly: communication, parenting, finances, even how we face adversity. We're not just reacting to life; we're co-creating it with purpose.

Alignment with my wife is vital to me because she's not just my partner, she's my best friend, my confidant, and my number one supporter. When we're on the same page spiritually, emotionally, and practically, our home becomes a place of strength and safety, not stress and confusion. It's how we model love and leadership to our children, and it's how we honor God in the covenant we made.

–CHRIS JOHNSON,
FOUNDER AND CEO, PASSIVE CANDIDATE PRO

USE A FULLY INVESTED FILTER[IP]

If you're Fully Invested, you guard your inputs—yours and your household's. What you watch, listen to, and talk about shows up in how you live. That's why, in our home, we don't watch television (except occasional sporting events) and are very careful with screentime in general. It's not punishment; it's protection of attention.

Input drives output. Stay close to people who challenge you to grow, not the ones who excuse staying the same or tell you what you want to hear. Limit your exposure to cynics and constant complainers who normalize quitting.

Run a *Fully Invested filter* on everything you read, watch, and ask yourself:

- Does it make you stronger, wiser, kinder, or more focused?
- Would you trade places with this person in the area they're teaching?
- Will you be glad you consumed this content a week from now?

If not, cut it. Your mind is a stage—cast it on purpose. Swap doom-scrolling and comment wars for deep work, a workout, a chapter of a great book, a date with your spouse, a walk with your kids, or quiet prayer.

Treat your brain like an elite athlete treats their body. Feed it quality. Protect recovery. Create whitespace. And don't let people with muddy shoes walk through your mind.

Guard the gate, and the rest of your life gets cleaner and faster.

Don't let people with muddy shoes walk through your mind.

SHARED VISION, STRONG MARRIAGE

Treat your marriage like a long-term investment, with strategic growth, alignment, and intentional nurturing. A strong marriage creates healthy people and better collaboration. My wife has her own pursuits (triathlons, extreme endurance races). I don't race; I support. Amber often attends big events and business conferences with me, especially when I'm giving a keynote speech. She also comes to some entrepreneurial retreats, especially the ones we host for our ELEVATED community. It's so much better to have her there with me than being at these events and conferences by myself. Giving each other room to chase our passions lets us thrive as individuals and bring that strength back to our marriage and parenting.

Many couples live side-by-side, not face-to-face. They trade updates on kids, schedules, and bills—but not on *each other*. That drift is quiet and becomes dangerous.

Disagreements aren't the problem; how you handle them is. At a couples conference, someone asked if we ever argue. Amber laughed: "Any couple who says they don't argue either never talks to each other or is lying." The goal isn't zero conflict—it's constructive conflict. You're two different people from two different backgrounds; of course, you'll clash. Repair fast. Offer respect during conflict, be quick with apologies, and offer shared solutions.

Chad and Amber, Kentucky Derby, 2025

Never be complacent, not in your life and not in your marriage. Complacency is one of my triggers. Amber and I are always looking to grow and get better, because there's always so much room where we can improve. We regularly talk about *us* and where we're headed.

A Fully Invested marriage is a shared mission, not just a shared address. Guard the voices that influence your home, and handle conflicts like a championship team.

A Fully Invested marriage is a shared mission, not just a shared address.

Over the years, my wife and I have learned to talk every day, and walk together if we can, give each other permission to start over, set goals, and dream together. We also read books on marriage and relationships together, say "sorry" often (and to be okay with being the first to do it), and go to couples' retreats and entrepreneurial events together to deepen our relationship.

We're still madly in love, after all these years! We certainly do not have the absence of disagreements or frustration. We just learned how to work through it. Here's to another thirty-five years!

—BRENT GROVE,
  REAL ESTATE AGENT

FULLY INVESTED FRAMEWORKS: CHOOSE YOUR PEOPLE

Make emotional deposits in your marriage through acts of service, words of affirmation, and date nights. Turning toward your significant other and connecting with them should be your default habit, not something you sometimes remember to do. For example, for my twenty-third wedding anniversary last year, I compiled this list of questions from a few different posts I saw online, typed it up, and brought it to our date at a nice steakhouse restaurant here in Newport Beach, California.

Yes, a printed paper of twenty-five questions.

If you want to try it, here's what I did:

1. Print the questions.
2. Book a nice restaurant.
3. Get all dressed up.
4. Order your food.
5. Put your phones in your pocket.
6. Answer each question, taking turns.
7. No judgment for answers.
8. Be open and honest.

Here's your "year in review" question list:

1. When did you feel the most loved by me?
2. When did you feel the most love for me?

3. What's one thing we've learned to appreciate more about each other?

4. Where do you think I've improved over the past year?

5. How have we supported each other's goals this year, and where can we offer more encouragement?

6. What's one thing you'd like to see more of in our relationship next year?

7. What would help you feel closer connected to me next year?

8. What did we handle very well together as parents this year?

9. What was the most challenging part of parenting for you?

10. Are there any new skills or values you want to focus on as a family next year?

11. How can I better support you in your role as a parent?

12. How did you feel about your physical health, mental health, and energy this year?

13. What positive health habits do you feel proud of this past year?

14. What's one thing we could do together to stay healthier in the new year?

15. What health habits are you most excited to work on individually in the coming year?

16. How has your faith grown or changed this year?

17. What have you done to increase your testimony and spirituality?

18. How can we expand our faith together and enhance our spirituality in the coming year, both as a couple and as a family?

19. What's your favorite memory together of us this year?

20. If you could relive one day this year, which day would it be and why?

21. What was unexpected this year that is something you're grateful for?
22. When were you most proud of me this year?
23. When were you most proud of yourself?
24. What's one experience you'd like to have together next year?
25. What would you love to say is true about us at the end of next year?

It took us two hours and fifteen minutes to finish our review, but the time went by quickly. We laughed, got teary-eyed, and learned something about each other. Give it a try!

CHALLENGE: THE RELATIONSHIP AUDIT

Purpose: Audit your closest relationships. Are they helping you grow or holding you back? Stop forcing relationships with people who don't reciprocate. Recognize that the wrong relationships aren't neutral; they actively drain your momentum.

Step 1: Do your current relationships lift you up or bring you down? Consider the people you interact with in real life as well as the social media accounts you follow.

Step 2: Don't just evaluate another person and whether they're aligned with your goals. Audit *yourself* and how you're showing up too. How can you be more Fully Invested in your most important relationships?

Why It Works: We don't grow unless we're honest with ourselves. To be a Fully Invested leader, you need to be choosy with your time and energy. This isn't being stingy; it's being intentional.

KEY TAKEAWAYS

- Whether in marriage or business, relationships don't last when one side is Fully Invested and the other is not. You must create a powerful network and inner circle of learners and thrivers.

- You may think you can't afford to terminate a high performer, but if they're undermining your culture, you can't afford to keep them.

- For me, the most important relationships are God, spouse, and then children. If you mess up those three, it's really hard to do well in the rest of your life. Everyone and everything else comes after.

- Input determines our output. Fully Invested leaders connect with those who challenge them to be better, not those who make excuses for staying the same or tell you what you want to hear.

- Many couples live side-by-side but not face-to-face. Don't fall into that trap. A Fully Invested marriage is a shared mission, not just a shared address. Be mindful of the voices that influence your marriage, and handle conflicts like a championship team.

CONCLUSION

You were sold the concept of a split life: work over here, family over there, "balance" somewhere in the fog between. It's a lie. You don't have two lives to juggle—you have *one* life to lead. When you live *Fully Invested*, business and home don't compete; they compound. Your marriage fuels your leadership. Your leadership blesses your marriage. Your standards don't change when you cross a threshold.

You already know this in your gut. The days you're present at home, your work sharpens. The weeks you lead with clarity at work, the calm shows up at the dinner table. Presence is the power. Alignment beats balance. One life. Many roles. Same standards.

> *Alignment beats balance. One life.*
> *Many roles. Same standards.*

And yes—this takes more than growth. It takes *transformation.* You don't want to become a bigger caterpillar; you want to become a bigger butterfly. Bigger output with the same identity only multiplies burnout. Transformation upgrades the identity, the operating system, and the rooms you choose.

If you're not Fully Invested, you're paying the hidden tax of being half-in, which causes drift, distraction, and distance from the people who matter most. Don't apologize for wanting an extraordinary marriage, an extraordinary family, and extraordinary results. Don't shrink your vision to fit someone else's story about what's "realistic." Excellence at home and excellence in business are not mutually exclusive. If we're truthful, they are mutually reinforcing.

Ideas are cheap. Execution is everything. If this book resonated with you, prove it with your calendar, your checkbook, your habits, and your proximity. Start now, not "when things slow down." Because they won't.

YOUR FULLY INVESTED PLAYBOOK^{IP}

In the Next 24 Hours:

- Schedule a *spouse huddle*: review calendars, money, priorities, gratitude, one friction to fix this week. Twenty minutes, phones down.
- Block two *deep-work windows* on your calendar. Guard them like revenue.
- Make one *proximity upgrade*: text a mentor or peer who stretches you and get on their calendar.

In the Next 30 Days:

- Book a *date night* and a *family experience* (not expensive, but intentional).
- Define *your five standards* at home and at work (on-time, tell the truth fast, no complaining without a proposed fix, stewardship of attention, fast repair after conflict, for example). Share them. Live them.
- Prune one *energy drain*—a commitment, habit, or relationship misfit. Replace it with one habit that compounds (sleep, training, reading, prayer).

In the Next 12 Months:

- Join or build the *room* you can't find: you want a circle where winning at work and winning at home are both required.
- Take a *vision retreat* with your spouse to cover faith, family, finances, health, or service. Set shared goals. Choose rituals that keep them alive.
- Codify *your operating system*: weekly reviews, quarterly resets, annual planning—with your family as the first team.

The Fully Invested Commitments

- I will choose *presence* over performance theater.
- I will protect *standards* before I protect feelings that excuse mediocrity.
- I will invest first in my *inner circle*—my spouse, my children, my core team.
- I will curate *proximity*—rooms that stretch me, not echo me.

- I will practice *fast repair*—own it quickly, fix it quickly, move forward together.
- I will say fewer, *deeper yeses* and many more *honest nos*.
- I will replace distraction with *devotion* to my mission, my marriage, my family, my calling.
- I will measure what matters and *tell the truth* about the results.
- I will lead one life with one set of *standards*, everywhere I go.

Success is simple, not easy. It's built on small, repeatable deposits made daily: at home and at work. Some people will close this book inspired and then drift back to default. Don't be that person. Build the life you say you want with the choices you make today and tomorrow and the day after that.

You get one life. Lead it *Fully Invested*: in your faith, your marriage, your family, your people, and your work. Love boldly. Protect your standards. Act before the damage spreads. And enjoy the compounding you unlock when you refuse to live a divided life.

Be Fully Invested—always.

ENDNOTES

1   Wigert, Ben and Corey Tatel. "The Great Detachment: Why Employees Feel Stuck." Gallup.com. December 3, 2024. https://www.gallup.com/workplace/653711/great-detachment-why-employees-feel-stuck.aspx.

2   "The Wise Man Built His House." featuring the Heritage Kids, track 3 on *All Are Precious in His Sight,* Gospel Heritage Foundation, 1997.

3   Willardson, Chad. "Here's Why Hustle Culture Is a Big Lie." *Entrepreneur.* February 3, 2023. https://www.entrepreneur.com/living/heres-why-you-need-to-move-away-from-hustle-culture/443227?fbclid=?AAabgJUj30tvjjr-tHWuiGjYaGeCVZe12ToBD4qF_6cr75QQVzOMtaHyThvg.

4   Billings, Josh. "Half of the troubles in this life." *Goodreads. com.* https://www.goodreads.com/quotes/550401-half-of-the-troubles-of-this-life-can-be-traced.

5   Ferriss, Tim. "The Not-to-Do List: 9 Habits to Stop Now." *Tim Ferris* (blog). August 16, 2007. https://tim.blog/2007/08/16/the-not-to-do-list-9-habits-to-stop-now/#:~:text=400%20comments,clear%20agenda%20or%20end%20time.

6   Eyal, Nir. "If you don't plan your day, someone or something else will." Accessed August 8, 2025. https://www.rocky.ai/leadership-quotes.

7   Rohn, Jim. "Never begin the day until it is finished on paper." *Facebook*. October 29, 2017. https://www.facebook.com/OfficialJimRohn/posts/never-begin-the-day-until-it-is-finished-on-paper-jim-rohn/10159493000235635/.

8   Robinson, Joe. "E-Mail Is Making You Stupid." Joe Robinson. March, 2010. Accessed July 27, 2025. https://www.worktolive.info/articles/bid/109951/E-Mail-Is-Making-You-Stupid.

9   Ramayya, Dr. Shreya, and Yi-Jin Yu. "Kids who own smartphones before age 13 have worse mental health outcomes: Study." *ABC News*. July 22, 2025. https://abcnews.go.com/GMA/Family/kids-smartphones-age-13-worse-mental-health-outcomes/story?id=123961082.

10   Ferris, Tim. "A person's success in life can usually be measured." *Goodreads.com*. Accessed August 5, 2025. https://www.goodreads.com/quotes/314019-a-person-s-success-in-life-can-usually-be-measured-by

11   Anderson, Jill. "The Benefit of Family Mealtime." Harvard Graduate School of Education. April 1, 2020. https://www.gse.harvard.edu/ideas/edcast/20/04/benefit-family-mealtime.

12   Comaford, Christine. "Are You Getting Enough Hugs?" *Forbes.com*. August 22, 2020. https://www.forbes.com/sites/christinecomaford/2020/08/22/are-you-getting-enough-hugs/.

13   Robbins, Tony. "Proximity is POWER!" Facebook.com. Accessed August 5, 2025. https://www.linkedin.com/posts/officialtonyrobbins_proximity-is-power-change-your-life-activity-7064258503225311232-1A3f.

14   "Find Your People," featuring Drew Holcomb & The Neighbors, track 2 on *Strangers No More*. Tone Tree Music. 2023.

ABOUT THE AUTHOR

Chad Willardson is the President and Founder of Pacific Capital, a wealth management business serving HNW entrepreneurs, based in Southern California. He's a certified member of the National Ethics Association and serves clients as a Certified Financial Fiduciary*, entrusted to manage money for families and businesses. Chad is featured in the Wall Street Journal, Forbes, U.S. News & World Report, CNBC, Investment News, Yahoo Finance, Inc., NASDAQ,

NBC News, Entrepreneur Magazine, and the California Business Journal. He is also the best-selling author of six books: *Stress Free Money, Smart, Not Spoiled, Fit for Wealth, Beyond the Money, Wealth Wired Differently, and Fully Invested.* He writes monthly articles for Entrepreneur and Forbes Business Council.

He also owns a growth-coaching business for entrepreneurs called ELEVATED. Chad and his wife, Amber, were married in San Diego, CA, back in 2001, and are the proud parents of five children. Service is part of their family culture. Chad is an Eagle Scout and served five years as a volunteer Scoutmaster in the Boy Scouts of America program and continues to be an involved leader for the Scouts. He earned the White House Volunteer Service Award in 2012 and appreciates the opportunity to make an impact through donating his time and resources to worthwhile causes both in the community and with the church his family attends. Chad also volunteered for a two-year service mission in Lithuania, Latvia, Estonia, and Belarus after his freshman year in college.

He graduated from Brigham Young University with a bachelor's degree in economics and a minor in business management. While at BYU, he worked directly with a portfolio manager responsible for $10 billion of investor funds. He also completed the two-year Financial Planning program at Boston University. Before founding Pacific Capital, Chad spent 9 years at Merrill Lynch, where he ranked in the top 2% of Financial Advisors nationally as a Senior Vice President and member of the Chairman's Club. He's guest lectured at M.I.T., B.Y.U., and Chapman University and has been designated a 5-Star Wealth Manager in both the Inland Empire and Orange County every year since 2012. He is also an Accredited Wealth Management Advisor and a Chartered Retirement Planning Counselor.

Chad grew up in Orange County, CA, and loves being in Southern California near family. You can learn more about him personally and professionally at ChadWillardson.com.

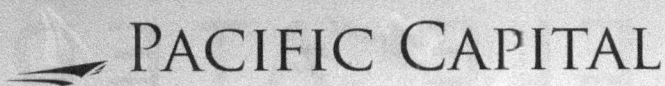

THIS BOOK IS PROTECTED INTELLECTUAL PROPERTY

Instant IP [IP]

The author of this book values Intellectual Property. The book you just read is protected by Instant IP[IP], a proprietary process, which integrates blockchain technology giving Intellectual Property "Global Protection." By creating a "Time-Stamped" smart contract that can never be tampered with or changed, we establish "First Use" that tracks back to the author.

Instant IP [IP] functions much like a Pre-Patent since it provides an immutable "First Use" of the Intellectual Property. This is achieved through our proprietary process of leveraging blockchain technology and smart contracts. As a result, proving "First Use" is simple through a global and verifiable smart contract. By protecting intellectual property with blockchain technology and smart contracts, we establish a "First to File" event.

Protected by Instant IP [IP]

LEARN MORE AT INSTANTIP.TODAY

www.ingramcontent.com/pod-product-compliance
Lightning Source LLC
Chambersburg PA
CBHW071553210326
41597CB00019B/3230